THE ABCs OɪEY

Painless Strategies for Ordinary People to Create Extraordinary Wealth

Dr Denis L. Cauvier
Alan Lysaght

Affiliate Offices: Singapore • London • New York • Toronto • Sydney • Vancouver
Malta • Paris • Johannesburg • Manilla • Hong Kong • Los Angeles

Fully Revised, updated version, copyright 2011.
Published by Wealth Solutions Press Inc.

First published in January 2003 by
Prentice Hall PTY Asia.

First North American publication, April 2003 by
Wealth Solutions Press Inc.

Second North American Printing, May 2003

Third North American Printing, September 2003

Fourth North American Printing, December 2003

Tenth North American Printing, February 2006

Twelfth North American Printing May 2010

Fourteenth North American printing April 2011

Printed in The United States
5   4   3   2   1
06   05   04   03
ISBN 0-9733549-0-9

This publication is designed to provide knowledgeable and depend-
able information regarding the subject matter covered; however, it is
sold with the understanding that the authors and publisher are not
engaged in rendering legal, financial or other professional advice.
Laws and practices vary from country to country and state to state,
and if legal or other expert assistance is required, the services of a
professional should be sought. The authors and publisher specifically
disclaim any liability that is incurred from the use or application of
the contents of this book.

International business consultants and professional speakers Dr. Denis Cauvier and Alan Lysaght bring out the psychological side of making money in this book... it is one of the best inspirational books to read and think about.

The Sunday Times, Singapore

From the bottom of my heart I thank you for writing this book. It will definitely help expand my business but more importantly it's about people helping people, and the first copy is definitely going to my son!

Dr. E.S. Baltimore, MD

You two guys nailed it on the head in easy to use steps. Follow the ABCs program and you will become wealthy.

P.R. Vancouver, Canada

This is one of the best books I've ever read....The whole book is fantastic!

J.B. Ottawa, Canada

You must hear this quite often but I want to personally thank you for providing me with the tools to immediately change my financial life.

Z.H. Topeka, KS

I just finished your book, and I have to say that it is excellent! It is an instant classic ranking right up there with, Think and Grow Rich, The Rich Dad series, and Wealth Without Risk.

D.S. Pittsburg, PA

Your book is fantastic. Everything is there: Goals, planning, inspiration, it is very, very, good. I have read countless financial books, and I haven't gotten as much out of them combined as I have from yours.

D.N. Tampa, FL

Received the book and just love it! So much of the content really hits home! My spouse was trying to get comfortable with our new business and after reading the book she feels so much more assured and committed to being an entrepreneur.

S.B. Los Angeles, CA

Your book is a simple translation of complicated financial concepts organized neatly from start to finish.

J.S. Manhattan, NY

Prior to reading your book I was one month away from losing my house, now I'm enjoying financial freedom and living the American dream.

S.L. Boston, MA

I am 11 years old and I am impressed with the common sense style of your book. Thanks to your book I now cut lawns and help seniors on my street. It feels great to earn and save MY OWN MONEY!

A.H. Seattle, WA

Buy this book today... use the ideas within today and you will never have to worry about your finances again!

B.C. Scottsdale, AZ

I never knew that making money and becoming wealthy was an option for me, I now have a very specific and logical wealth plan thanks to your book.

M.Z. Denver, CO

I love your book. It's full of tangeable "Can-use-today" material. It has literally changed my life.

D.C. London, England

If you are serious about your future buy this book!

K.S. Palm Springs, CA

As a high school educator I encourage all of my students to read your invaluable book.

L.L. Detroit, MI

Your book is like a distillation of the top 20 financial books of all time expressed in the most inspirational, common-sense language.

M.J. Farmington Hills, Il

MONEY BACK GUARANTEE!

We are so confident in the wealth building strategies outlined in this book that we are offering a full money back guarantee as follows:

If, after reading - and adopting - the wealth building Attitudes and Behaviors outlined in this book, you do not **make or save at least 100 times the purchase price** of this book in the first year, we will happily refund your money... and, you still get to keep the book. (Please save your receipt).

The ABC Guys

TABLE OF CONTENTS

Acknowledgements

Denis: There are so many people to thank, so many friends, mentors, peers, suppliers and clients. First and foremost, I acknowledge the sacrifice that the three ladies of my life have made during the period of researching and writing this book. Debbie, Sam and Stevie, I love you forever, I love you for always. A special thanks goes to one of my mentors Bill Gibson who has always been there for me.

Alan: Thanks are due to M.G. Lysaght and to Lynn, Chrissy and Rachel; each of whom were inspirational in their own ways in the writing of this book.

We would also like to acknowledge the hundreds of self-made millionaires that shared so openly their experiences and advice.

We both owe a debt of gratitude to the fabulous Prentice Hall Singapore team who helped in the Asian version of this book. Special thanks to the Marketing team for making it a bestselling book in record time.

For the American edition we want to thank George Foster for the cover art.

For their help in making us feel relaxed and comfortable during our various writing sessions, the Sandals Resorts chain.

During our many travels, many people both rich and poor, shared their stories and experiences with us. Many we were able to help with some suggestions, while others provided useful learning lessons for this book. We thank them all.

Through our seminars we have met many wonderful people, too numerous to mention, some of whom have provided good examples and suggested financial problem areas common to others that needed to be examined. They have all been a great help and this book is stronger for their input. You know who you are.

INTRODUCTION

Becoming wealthy is not a mysterious or secret process. Considering how important it is to our lives, it is really surprising how little time we devote to learning about it. Everybody manages to learn at least one language. Many people learn how to use something complicated such as a computer or a car. If you can learn those things then you can learn how to become wealthy.

Most people have abilities and skills that they are not using to their financial benefit. Many of the people we've met in the process of our consulting business work day-to-day in jobs that take all their time and energy, and which end up leaving them living below the poverty line when they retire. At the same time they have a passion for something that could make them wealthy. Our job is to help people recognize their talents and achieve financial success. Suggesting new ways of organizing financial lives, or opening people's minds to alternative ways of setting up their businesses to take advantage of the assets they already have, is what we do and the reason we have written this book.

We are presenting two ways to accumulate wealth. The first is conservative, takes place over time and is virtually painless, even fun. To accomplish this we will walk you through the steps to a new understanding of wealth, show you how to properly assess your current situation and how to better organize your financial life for the long term. For many people financial matters are scary and mysterious, so we will go slowly and make things very simple and pain free. If you follow these steps you will be significantly richer over time. When you start to gain more financial independence and increase your confidence level, you may choose to pursue some of the ideas in the last part – Section C – and live the life of the rich and famous.

The second system, presented in Section C, is more aggressive. It is a much shorter path to wealth and one in which you will need a slightly stronger stomach. The first step here is to learn to appreciate the assets you already have. Then we show specifically, through very relatable stories, how you can make a fortune doing what you love. If you are impatient and want us to "show you the money" now, you can skip right to Section C and get started but we recommend reading the first two sections so that you learn the secrets of keeping the money once you get it.

If you apply even one thing you learn in this book you will easily make back 100 times its cost. If you take the lessons from this book the least bit seriously, you will dramatically change your life-style, make thousands of dollars you would not otherwise have made and positively change the future for yourself and those you care about. If you use the material in this book aggressively and are prepared to do some work, you should become wealthy fairly quickly.

These are not "get rich quick" schemes. Everything is 100 per cent legal. Following these suggestions will not stretch the tax laws in any way. On the contrary, you will learn to use them for your benefit rather than always paying the tax department. These are tried and true strategies that we have been using and learning from for years.

We gained these insights into wealth generation from decades of research and experience with self-made millionaires. We have shared the information with individuals in one-on-one consulting, couples, large groups in training programs, half- and full-day seminars and multi-day retreats. We have also provided strategic corporate solutions to senior executive teams to create competitive advantages and greater profits. Over the years certain themes and lessons kept reappearing. They are consistent and they are not rocket science. They are the principles upon which this book is based.

ANYONE CAN BE RICH

Despite the worst recession since the great Depression, the world has churned out more new self-made millionaires than at any other time in history. After conducting extensive research and interviews we were surprised to learn that this fortunate group includes very few with any serious financial education, either academic or otherwise. Fewer still inherited their wealth and an almost insignificant number came by their fortune by way of lotteries or "Lady Luck."

In other words, the profile of this group looks a lot like the average person. These people do not have extraordinary talents and are no different from you. They simply make savvy, informed choices regarding money and, more than anything else, they believe in themselves.

The purpose of this book is to show you, first of all, that you can actually become rich if you have the right attitude. Then, as clearly as possible, we will show you the tried and true methods employed by rich people everywhere in maintaining their wealth.

Do you really want to make money? Do you know what you would do with wealth if you achieved it? As you will see when you read this book, the technical steps are surprisingly simple. In fact, one of the biggest roadblocks to becoming wealthy is a person's attitude.

Have you ever said "I am no good with money," "I live pay check to pay check, there is no way I can start a savings plan" or "Investing is too complicated. I will figure it out when I am older." A lot of people find finances too confusing to think about and hope that someday, if they keep working themselves up the company hierarchy, things will work out. They will not. Statistically, you are almost certain to live in poverty when you retire. And, you are no different from millions of other people.

Most financial books we have read are geared to those with a strong financial background. *The ABCs of Making Money* is designed for those without a financial background, who know what they want and are prepared to take those initial steps towards financial independence.

There are three very important things that you will learn by the time you finish this book. The first is how to use the money you currently earn much more efficiently. Second, that even someone who cannot read financial reports can invest and make money in the stock markets and third, that following your passion and doing what you have always wanted to do in life can make you both rich and happy.

As you will read in Chapter 1, a negative attitude towards wealth creation is the single biggest stumbling block in its attainment. Many people labor under the mistaken belief that being wealthy is something that only happens to others. Well, if you think you can't obtain it, you won't! It sounds simple, but to achieve anything, including the accumulation of wealth, you must fully believe in yourself or you will never be completely successful. This is not just some new-age catch-phrase. Winning attitudes are the precondition for every form of human success. The most successful businesses have learned to hire only people with winning attitudes. If you want to have a successful personal relationship, both partners have to have winning attitudes. You may also have noticed that the healthiest people tend to have the most positive attitudes. When you put your mind to work on a positive strategy the results can be really overwhelming. This is the reason we begin this book examining our attitudes and providing steps to change them. Chapter 1 will cite examples of people who have enjoyed success after simply changing their attitudes. The money-saving or money-generating strategies that follow in Sections B and C of this book are proven, practical tools to help you achieve your desired life-style.

Throughout this book you will read many easy strategies to save money. Simple, step-by-step instructions will show you how to reposition your mortgage and consolidate credit-card debts and how saving as little as $25 every week can change your economic life substantially in just a few years. And, be assured that you do not have to live like a pauper to save thousands of dollars.

You may find yourself thinking that all this talk about creating wealth is great but "Right now I am a little busy and I will get to this financial stuff a little later." Consider this: Only 8% of Americans retiring at age 65 live above the poverty line! Only 2 - 4% retire to the same standard of living they enjoyed while they were working.

Poverty is a degrading dehumanizing, cancer-like disease of the uninformed mind.

– Mark Victor Hansen,
Author of *Chicken Soup For The Soul*

Too many people are hurting as a result of financial pressures, unable to retire with a decent life-style, feeling the relentless stress of debt burdens, watching helplessly as an unending parade of advertising shows them the things they cannot afford. Too many people are forced to turn to their children and say "Maybe next year kids," feeling that despite how hard they try, the whirlpool of financial despair is constantly dragging them under.

This is clearly unacceptable so we did some research and found the reasons for this sad statistic. It turns out that for most of the people surveyed, financial planning simply never occurred to them. Others said they "just plain procrastinated." Some admitted that they were unable to delay "instant gratification" while the rest said they had no long-term perspective.

There is a very simple, low-cost solution to this problem and it involves time. Saving money seems to become a bigger preoccupation for people the closer they get to celebrating their 65th birthday. Unfortunately, at that point, they have pretty much run out of wealth building time. Here is a simple example of how big a factor time plays with your savings. If you start putting $100 every month into a savings account when you are 55 years old, (assuming you get an average eight per cent interest) you will have $18,417 when you retire. If you started that savings plan only ten years earlier at age 45 you would have $59,295 when they hand you your gold watch. Starting your plan at age 35 would net you $149,036 and, if you were smart enough to begin when you were 25, you would have $349,101 when you retire and need it the most. In the chapter on investing we will show you how to take this simple strategy one painless step further and increase that nest egg to over one million dollars! Obviously the earlier you start to take control of your financial destiny the better. Buying this book was the first and smartest step on this journey. If you take the information in this book seriously, there is a good chance that you will be enjoying yourself at the Country Club when you retire.

Many people believe that they cannot be rich because they do not have "the smarts," did not get a great education, do not have a business degree or lack training in marketing, so they just give up. Actually, we all have incredible training in marketing. We see it all around us every day of the week. We are constantly bombarded by images in magazines and on television asking us to buy something. We innately know which ones work and which ones do not. We are here to tell you that there are some very simple things you can do without any training, education or courses to become much more successful and, if you work at it, rich.

The following table illustrates the savings that can be made by simple changes in some common bad habits.

The Average Adult VS The Money Magnet

The Average Adult	The Money Magnet (MM)	MM's result in 30 years
Cannot save extra money	Puts $50 per week into mutual funds paying ten per cent	Saves $494,721.62
Pays minimum monthly on a $250,000 30-year mortgage at 7.5 per cent	Invests extra $268 per month on mortgage	Saves $143,086.80 and ten years of payments
Pays minimum due on on credit cards (average balance is $1,000 on all cards)	Pays credit cards in full every month	Saves $7,525
Buys new wardrobe with unexpected $500 bonus	Invests bonus in mutual funds paying ten per cent	Saves $82,247.01
Eats $10 lunch out twice every week	Limits eating to one lunch (invests dollars saved at ten per cent)	Saves $98,944.33
Smokes cigarettes, one pack per day	Quits smoking (invests dollars saved at ten per cent)	Saves $440,491.50
Renews insurance policies automatically	Shops for the best car, home and life insurance	Saves $8,200

Pays late charges on bill payments	Pays bills on time	Saves $3,700
Ignores suggestions to reduce heating or air-con costs by insulating home	Insulates home, turns off unused lights, instals thermostats, energy-efficient heater	Saves $8,891
Pays full price on clothing	Buys clothes on sale (preseason or end of season sale)	Saves $4,854

Total money saved	$1,292,661.23
Plus appreciated value of mortgage-free home (Assuming 1.5 per cent appreciation per year)	$435,283.61
Net worth	$1,727,944.83

Even if you make only one or two of these changes, which are described in more detail later on in the book, you will be substantially ahead of your current situation.

For most people, balancing their check books every month is a happy accomplishment. They owe money on their credit cards and pay the minimum possible on their mortgages once a month. These people owe it to themselves to visit the opulent corporate headquarters of their banks and credit-card companies. After all, they pay for them every month. Why not take your share of corporate excess and put it in your own pocket. You can. It is legal and not very complicated. Why is it that more people do not do it? The answer for many is that they are scared. They say "It is too complicated" and "I do not know how to do stuff like that."

We want to show you in this book that you do not have to be afraid. Banks are not smarter than you, they just do not tell you the whole story when they, for example, sell you a mortgage. On a $250,000 mortgage over 25 years at 7.5 per cent, your cost of borrowing would be $298,517 (that is on top of the $250,000 principal). You could cut that cost down by almost $100,000 ($96,971) simply by making your payments weekly instead of monthly. That way you keep the money you saved in your pocket, or better yet, put it into a profitable investment and let the bank make you rich. Would you do that if we took you through the incredibly simple steps one at a time? Of course you would. If you follow these easy strategies you will be smacking yourself in the head one year from now for not doing this sooner.

Denis and Alan's definition of wealth:

Having what you want, and wanting what you have.

We are not reinventing the wheel or teaching mysterious secrets. These are basic truths that, unfortunately, the vast majority of people do not know. If you are not rich and would like to be and you are prepared to do a little work, we can show you how to change your life.

If you follow the steps outlined in this book and refer to the free resources which are included in our website, www. abcguys.com, we cannot guarantee that you will be a millionaire one year from now because people move at their own pace and some will cover the ground quicker than others. But, can we guarantee that you will be substantially richer a year from now? *Absolutely!* Read on.

Note to readers outside America: We refer to "IRAs" throughout the book. This is essentially the same as a Registered Retirement Savings Plan (RRSP).

Section I

—— ❧❧❧ ——

Attitudes for Making Money

1

Your Attitude to Wealth Can Cost You Millions or Make You Millions

Do you deserve to be rich? This may seem like a silly question but many people are unsure of their answer. A negative attitude towards wealth creation, as with most important things in life, is the single biggest stumbling block in its attainment. If, deep down, you think you can't obtain it, you won't. As simple as this truth is, it is surprisingly pervasive. It is the reason we begin this book examining our attitudes and providing steps to change them. We are not certain but it may even be the reason the alphabet was designed to start with the letter A. And, as you will see in this chapter, the learning principle is exactly the same as when we first learned the alphabet as a child. A person has to understand A before he or she is capable of getting to B and C.

If you follow all the money-saving or money-generating strategies in Sections B and C of this book you will be well on your way to a fabulous life-style. Without examining and, if necessary, realigning your attitude towards wealth, your success will be something akin to peddling a bicycle with its chain off the main sprocket. Sheer friction will ultimately propel you forward but nowhere near as quickly or efficiently as if your beliefs and attitudes are aligned and in sync. Identifying, and then sorting out any problems in this area will make the rest of the strategies much easier to achieve and much more successful.

> Sooner or later, those who win are those who think they can.
>
> – Richard Bach,
> Author of *Jonathan Livingston Seagull*

Many people get the idea to start exercising or to quit smoking then give up after a few days. Was the idea wrong? No. Unfortunately, their attitude did not support their idea. Until you have completely committed to the idea of giving up cigarettes in your head, you are likely to fail. There are thousands of unused rowing and running machines gathering dust in basements for the same reason. Making money also demands commitment. It is not nearly as hard as quitting smoking or going to the gym three days a week, but it does take focus. That is why we are devoting this time to first refining your attitude towards money. We do not want to see this book sitting beside your unused aerobics machine. Life is too short so why not enjoy it from the seats in First Class?

When you think about the words *wealth* and *money* what thoughts immediately come into your mind? Are all these thoughts positive?

In the space provided below take the time to write down the first five beliefs surrounding money and wealth that come into your head.

_____

_____

_____

Have you ever heard any of these attitudes about wealth and money?

- Money does not grow on trees.
- Money cannot buy happiness.

- If you are rich you must be selfish.
- The love of money is the root of all evil.
- You have to pay your dues.
- Wealthy people are unhappy.
- Wealth corrupts.
- It takes lots of money to make money.
- Wealthy people never enjoy happy relationships.
- You have to be born into money.

How many of these beliefs are negative? Here is another perspective. If you ask a citrus grower they will tell you that in fact money actually does grow on trees. The pulp and paper industry would also agree. Take a look at the paper currency in your pocket; it came from a tree.

One of the most common myths that we hear over and over as we travel the world is: Money cannot buy happiness. Well, that is partially true, but you sure can rent it for the night – a good video, for example. Contrary to popular belief it does not take a lot of money to make money. Take the low cost of this book, add a little self discipline and creativity and wealth is yours.

If you buy into the beliefs in the above list they will hold you back from making money. Now, review your list of five beliefs and try to remember who was responsible for programming them. Did they have money problems? Ask yourself if any of these people are or were wealthier than you. Would you take the advice of an auto mechanic on a medical question or ask a doctor to fix your car? Most people would not, yet it is surprising how many people accept financial advice from people who have very little money. Our research has shown that people who have negative attitudes about wealth are generally people who do not have much money. When we need a solution to a problem, we approach the most qualified person we can afford. That way we are likely to get a longer-term, or even permanent, solution to the problem.

Think about how your attitudes about wealth and money have shaped your current financial situation. Are all of them positive? If not, ask yourself what your life would look like if you replaced all your negative and limiting wealth beliefs with positive ones. The answer for most people is: **financial abundance**.

Before going any further it would make sense to take some time and come up with your own personal definition of wealth. A dictionary defines wealth as: The state of being rich; great abundance of anything. That may mean money or it may mean health and being surrounded by loved ones. Write your own definition in the space provided below.

My Definition of Wealth

_____

_____

_____

_____

Now that you have created a definition of wealth you are more likely to achieve it than those who do not have one. This brings up the question: Why are some people more financially successful than others? It is a very interesting question. We all know of people who were born in the same town, raised in the same neighborhood, had the same basic education and upbringing, the same kind of family structure – yet one person appeared to become wildly successful while others did not. But by whose standards? Success is intrinsically personal. By some standards a person is successful if he or she becomes a corporate executive, a good parent, a wonderful person, a proactive manager or an accomplished artist.

There are several reasons why some people are more successful than others:

1. Successful people have a clear personal mission which steers their actions in life.
2. They have a positive mental attitude, which helps them "know" they will achieve their goals.
3. They are willing to make sacrifices to achieve success.
4. They are persistent. As Sir Winston Churchill so eloquently put it, "Never give up; never, never give up!"
5. The most successful people have set meaningful and challenging goals for themselves.

6. They have made a conscious effort to focus on these goals and have a specific plan of action for bringing them to reality.
7. They work towards their goals; every single day they take specific actions towards achieving them.

So, what is success? How does it happen? Is success something that is inborn, genetic or hereditary? Is it environmentally developed? Is there a global definition, or is it purely one's perspective of oneself? How can you become more successful? These are age-old questions. In this book, we will examine each of these points in the hope of giving you a map for your success.

Before you achieve more success in life, you have to know what success means to you. Ask yourself the questions: What are all the positives in my life?, What is my life missing? and What is my purpose in life? To be successful, you must have a very clear understanding of what your life's mission is. Once you have established your Personal Life Mission Statement you are on your way to identifying your path to success.

My Personal Life Mission Statement

_____

_____

_____

Now that you have your definition of wealth and you have designed a Personal Life Mission Statement, the next step is to write down what success represents to you. It is often a combination of wealth and personal goals. Remember that the acquisition of wealth is only a tool towards gaining success. Money is an amplifier. Money amplifies the true person. Nice people, who become rich, simply become nice rich people. They use wealth as a tool to help themselves, their families and other people. When people who are mean spirited become rich, they then have the means to become really nasty. At the risk of sounding preachy it is important to look beyond wealth to the other important issues in life.

My Personal Definition of Success

_____

_____

_____

We believe that success means being completely happy with your life, as it is now and with the direction in which you are going. By clearly defining what success means to you personally – whether it is having a million dollars in the bank, being able to play golf twice a week, having more time for your family and friends or giving more of your time and effort to a favorite charity – you have created a target. If you have not taken the time to define your target, opportunities can be lost because you are not focused enough to recognize them as fundamental to your success.

Imagine for a moment an Olympic medallist in archery who is asked to hit a target for a million-dollar prize. The person knows all the technical steps and is very confident of their victory. Just before shooting, however, two intriguing things happen. A hood is placed over the archer's head and they are spun around three times. What do you think the result would be? The archer would be lucky to come anywhere close to the target! Why? Because **you can't hit a target you can't see!**

The same principle is at work in becoming wealthy. You may know all the technical steps for success: have a good degree, a good job, a good network of contacts and you have read this book from cover to cover, but unless you can see your target you will remain unfocused, disoriented and never really know if you've achieved success. Now that you have defined your expectations for wealth, you have made a Personal Life Mission Statement and have a definition of success, you have effectively taken off your "blindfold" and have a target at which to aim.

One of the things you may discover as a result of this exercise is that you do not need millions of dollars to achieve your success. This may mean less dramatic changes in your current life-style. We know a woman who retired at age 39. After 15 years in a high-stress executive position she sold her mostly paid-for big city condominium apartment and moved to a cottage in a small community where her only expenses are heat, hydro and some small property taxes. She lives very frugally from the modest interest in her investment plan. She grows her own fruit and vegetables and spends most of her days painting. For a little extra income, but mostly because she likes to, she teaches art to children. She was in the fortunate position of having been a good saver and aggressively paid down her mortgage while she could afford to.

She calculated that since the majority of her income went to pay taxes and the maintenance of her career – designer clothes, prestige car, etc. – if she stopped working she could eliminate most of her expenses and live on very little. For her, personal time is her most valuable commodity. She now considers herself hugely successful. For others, money is very important. There is nothing wrong with that, you just have to be prepared to make more dramatic changes in your current spending and savings habits to achieve that goal.

Now, ask yourself, "Is what I'm doing on a day-to-day basis consistent with the direction I want to go and the goals I want to achieve? Is it taking me closer to my vision of success?" If you find that your day-to-day habits are actually detracting from your mission, you can either:

a. Change your mission.
b. Change your day-to-day habits.
c. Accept mediocrity.

Accepting mediocrity is not a very positive choice, so you need to decide whether your daily activities are of greater importance than your mission. In order to be successful, you may have to change some activities in your life such as starting a new business or learning to save and invest.

> I was convinced that if you thought poor, you stayed poor, and I had no intention of staying that way.
>
> – Ray Kroc,
> Founder of McDonalds Restaurants

ATTITUDES AND SELF-CONCEPTS

Another extremely important piece of information you need to understand is your self-concept. This is fuelled by information you start to receive the day you are born. In subtle increments, the way your parents, family, friends, teachers and co-workers treat and react to you, form your feelings about yourself. Let's say your parents had little time for you as you grew up. Perhaps they encouraged you to go play somewhere else so that they could read the paper when you wanted to play or cuddle. If that happened often, it would begin to register in your mind that you must not be very important, otherwise they would want to play with you. If you had a habit of accidentally knocking things over to which they responded, "Don't be so stupid; look where you're going!" that too would register. This kind of instruction eventually tells you that you are not very bright. After all, your own parents told you so. This starts to become a self-fulfilling prophecy. Today, child psychologists stress the importance of these often-unintended parental messages. Luckily, in most cases parents balance off these comments, made in moments of frustration, with equally positive messages.

An interesting series of studies was conducted by Yale University to examine the types of messages being sent out to adolescents by the average North American family. In a large sample testing over a seven-day period, the messages were: 32 positive and 431 negative! That is bound to have an impact on how anyone sees the world.

It is important to understand that whether positive or negative, all these messages register and they all have an effect on how you operate as an adult. Let's take a concrete example – Denis' career as a public speaker. Having spoken in front of more than one million people in 45 countries over a span of 20 years, you might expect that he was positively motivated towards speaking in front of crowds his whole life, but that is not the case.

In his words: "In elementary school I was chosen to come up to the front and answer some basic multiplication questions. After several wrong answers, I began to hear the chuckles from my classmates. As I headed back to my seat I thought

'Denis, how could you be so stupid? Even a six-year-old would know those answers!' This was one of my first public speaking experiences and, down in my subconscious mind, a new file was opened called Public Speaking. The information in that newly created file indicated that Public Speaking was a not-so-favorable experience. The next time this happened was in geography class. I got up in front of the class to talk about Central Africa. I knew the material well but just before I spoke, my conscious mind, registering the eyes looking at me in anticipation, said to my subconscious 'Hey, Denis, what do you remember about Public Speaking?' The report came back 'You are not very good at it.'

"Because I used past performance for directions and guidance to my current performance, I had the confident expectation that I would not do well. As actions are always consistent with dominant thoughts, I started to stammer. I got nervous, forgot the material and walked back to my seat amid a chorus of snickers and jeers. This is an example of a self-fulfilling prophecy. It was not that I was bad. I told myself that I was bad and then lived out that belief. This additional failure planted more negative reinforcement in my subconscious and I continued in a downward spiral.

"By the time I arrived at high school I refused to volunteer for any speaking in front of the class because I was convinced, based on past information, that I would make a fool of myself. I would answer teachers' questions by saying, 'I don't know!' even though I knew the answer (that's my story)! During graduation year I thought I could overcome my past habits and prepared a speech for the whole school. Everything was fine until I got up in front of the assembly, heard the expectant silence, felt the eyes locking on to me and the wave of terror washing over me. Once again I had the real expectation that I was going to blow it. For no other reason my voice got shaky, knees got weak, hands got sweaty and my stomach leapt up to my throat. You can imagine the rest, including the vow to never again try public speaking."

In survey after survey, people consistently rank public speaking as their number one fear, even ahead of dying. (Following this logic, if someone tells you that you are going to die you should feel relieved. After all it could be worse; they could have asked you to give a speech.) It is likely, therefore, that many of you can relate to this example. Happily we can report that things have changed dramatically in Denis' public-speaking abilities, which should give you confidence to continue reading and learn how to correct your own erroneous life scripts.

Does this story resonate with you? Have you picked up any self-limiting beliefs over the years? Write down five of the things you hate or fear the most concerning money. The list may include anything, but for our purposes try thinking of job or finance-related phobias, such as speaking to your boss or workgroup, being your own boss or speaking to a bank manager about a loan.

Looking over your list, try and trace back the origin of each of your discomforts. Are they based on a previous bad experience? If this is the case, ask yourself this question: "What would happen if I no longer saw each of these items in a negative light? If I started to look forward with excitement to each of these activities, would it make a positive difference in my life?" If this is the case then it may be time to reprogram parts of your self-concept. (This, by the way, will work equally well with other aspects of your life such as dating or trying new activities.) This is not always an easy process but the payoff will be more than worthwhile. Take a drive by that BMW dealer while you are thinking about it.

Positive Affirmation Statements

When we last heard from Denis he was in a bad way. He was a victim of bad previous messages. How did he go from the high level of pain associated with public speaking, to thoroughly enjoying the experience, earning awards and extraordinary fees? The answer is actually very simple: He changed his association to speaking from one of pain to one of pleasure.

"I began a series of very easy mental, emotional and physical exercises. Physically, I took the time to handwrite a good speech. The mental part required more effort as I had to reprogram my subconscious mind to associate speaking in front of an audience with pleasurable feelings. The tool for this is called

Positive Affirmation Statements which, in reality, is nothing more than giving yourself a pep talk. Instead of reinforcing my subconscious belief that I was a lousy public speaker I started to say to myself that I was now a great public speaker. By saying this over and over to myself I was gradually able to reprogram my subconscious mind to become comfortable with the idea of being a good speaker. This may sound unrealistically simple but remember my problem was not *what* I had to say, it was the self-sabotage coming from my subconscious.

"I also linked positive emotions to public speaking. Instead of linking feelings of embarrassment, failure and disappointment and maybe even thoughts of being ridiculed to public speaking I decided to think of something pleasurable: for me it was downhill skiing. Simply saying 'downhill skiing' automatically triggered a series of positive emotions. I took a favorite skiing poster, hung it in my office and then said to myself, 'Public speaking, I love it' while staring at the poster.

"Eventually, when I thought about public speaking, my mind conjured up the picture of the skier which led to positive thoughts and feelings. The next time I got up in front of a group of people and saw them staring back at me, my mind checked the file on 'Public Speaking' and it told me that this was a really enjoyable activity and that I was 'a great public speaker.' Now I was free to concentrate on the material in my speech rather than on how I was going to undermine myself. After completing a few practice speeches, which reinforced my new beliefs positively, I was able to launch a very lucrative and successful speaking career."

The point of this whole story as it relates to wealth creation is that **your past does not need to equal your future**. It may be as simple as changing your perspective. However, failure to recognize any dangerous negative, self-fulfilling prophesies will lead to dire financial outcomes. These self-limiting beliefs account for more of the casualties along the road to wealth creation than all the bad investments combined. Over the years we have met countless people that have been held back financially because of some unfounded fear. The most common financial fears that we hear around the world are:

- With the economy as it is I am afraid of losing my job.
- My boss intimidates me so much I cannot bring myself to ask for the raise I am owed.
- I would love to own my own house, but real estate can be too risky and if the housing market drops I will lose my life savings.
- I am dissatisfied with the interest generated from my savings account but I fear losing it all in another stock market crash.
- I want to search for a better job, but if my present company finds out that I am looking I will be fired.
- The better opportunities are in another part of the country, but it will require leaving my friends and family behind.
- I know there is great money to be made in professional selling but all that rejection really scares me.
- I feel that the cost is more than we can afford, but if I try to negotiate on price, I could lose out on buying our dream home.
- All my life I have wanted to own a business and to be my own boss but everyday the media reports about all the business failures and I cannot afford to lose everything.

The fear that is expressed in these statements causes very real emotional pain for those who have these thoughts. The pain can be so overwhelming that it prevents the individual from doing what they so passionately desire. The key is to get clear on what your priorities are and ask yourself why you want something before worrying about how you will achieve it. If you do not have a very compelling reason for why you want it, then it is impossible to justify the mental and physical effort required to overcome the fear.

The root cause of all fear is ignorance. Therefore, the cure for finance-related fears is knowledge. It is no different than curing the fear of the dark, fear of flying, fear of heights, etc. The answer comes through knowledge. So the trick is to take the principles offered in Chapter 1 and 2 of this book and apply them to your smaller fears, conquer them, celebrate and then move on to conquer bigger fears as your bank accounts grow.

THREE COMMON FEAR SITUATIONS

"My boss intimidates me so much I cannot bring myself to ask for the raise I feel I am owed."

Alan relates a story of a woman named Maya. "Inspired by what she heard in one of my seminars, she approached me with her story of how she had overcome her natural fear of approaching people to gain more specific information. Maya was an office worker who loved her job and believed that she was very good at it. She had been at her current job for eight years, liked her coworkers and suppliers and believed that she deserved more money.

"Sitting over a coffee I walked her through a simple exercise to help her understand her value to the company. On one side of the balance sheet she represented a $30,000 cost to her employer. Fortunately the other side had a longer list.

1. She fulfilled all of the functions for which she was originally hired.
2. There had been very little adjustment in salary for inflation over the years.
3. She regularly attended Association meetings on her own time which allowed for good networking. These contacts resulted in roughly $50,000 worth of new sales leads to her company. Even though others closed the sales, at a 15 per cent profit margin she had initiated $7,500 worth of net profit for the company.
4. She had begun doing the bookkeeping for the company, allowing them a net savings of $15,000 per year by not renewing the contract of the independent bookkeeper they had been using.
5. She designed a series of improvements to the inventory control system, which resulted in an average annual savings of $11,000 in carrying costs.
6. Keeping her employed helped the company avoid hiring and retraining costs.

"Maya started to see the value she represented to her employer. She was bringing in or saving the company at least $30,000 per year, on top of fulfilling all the functions for which she was originally hired. All she really wanted was a $5,000 raise to help her pay off some debts and establish a savings plan. She was still intimidated by the thought of approaching her boss so I asked her to identify his single biggest concern. Her immediate response? 'Profit.' 'Well, looking at it don't you think that the balance sheet approach would resonate easily with him?' 'Yes, but he could still choose to fire me.'

"'Look again at all of the positives you came up with. If he does not see the advantages of rewarding you then he is not a very astute businessman. Think about what it would cost him to replace you. If he is smart he will understand that instead of penalizing you, he should be encouraging you to do more networking and give you increased responsibilities through which you will both profit. The other crucial thing to consider is that your list of positives would be very attractive to another employer. You need and deserve to have more confidence in yourself.'

"'He currently represents someone with more power than you. Let's flip the paradigm around now and think about your power in the situation. When you go in to speak with him that is the position you want to be speaking from. It is not arrogance; it is a matter of believing in yourself and your abilities. If you don't see the value you represent, then how do you expect him to see it? It can mean the difference between failure and a raise.' Maya got the raise and shortly thereafter, a promotion."

"I would love to own my own house but real estate can be too risky and if the market drops I will lose my life savings."

Making a monthly deposit to someone else's retirement fund in the form of rent just doesn't make much sense. Virtually no real estate will drop in value to zero unless you find yourself on top of a toxic waste dump, in which case the government will probably be embarrassed into moving you to a better neighborhood. Historically, real estate has always appreciated over time. Remember the three keys to buying a house: location, location and location. Even the most valuable mutual funds or stocks will not keep you warm or dry at night. We've heard all the arguments for and against buying a home and, on balance, you are almost certainly going to come out further ahead if you buy rather than rent. What the sub-prime mortgage meltdown taught people (hopefully!) is the importance of getting reliable information before signing up for escalating payments they may not be able to afford later on. Chapter 4 will deal with the tricks for house/condominium financing in greater detail.

"All my life I have wanted to own a business and be my own boss, but everyday the media reports about all the business failures. I cannot afford to lose everything."

On the contrary, owning your business can offer you more job security than a regular job. As the business owner you have more control over your future and your rewards are tied directly to your efforts. Working for someone can still leave you vulnerable to layoffs or missed promotions and you are leaving your destiny in someone else's hands.

The key to starting a successful business is good research and proper preparation. Section C of this book will prepare you for some of the situations you will face. Of course businesses fail. You cannot plan for everything but even if your business fails you will learn from the experience, which will put you in a much better position the next time you try. It took Thomas Edison over 2,000 tries before he perfected the invention of the lightbulb. When someone asked him how he dealt with all those failures he said, "What failures? I thought of each experience as a valuable learning lesson."

> The way to double your success rate is to double your failure rate.
>
> – Tom Watson,
> President, IBM

The main point here is that the person who has a lot of positive feelings about himself or herself and enjoys a healthy level of self-esteem will also have the confidence to move forward in life. These feelings are directly tied to your actions. As actions produce results, at the most basic level, your degree of success depends on how positive you feel about yourself.

EXPECTATIONS

There was a famous study done here in America where researchers took an average group of teachers and gave them an average group of students. The teachers were told they were part of an elite experiment and were selected for the study because of their gifted teaching abilities. They were also told that the students were hand-selected for their classes because they were extraordinarily bright. The teachers and students were asked not to discuss the experiment with anyone. By the end of the year, these classes had the highest grade point averages in the entire city! When the teachers were told that, in fact, their students were only average at the beginning of the year, they claimed the success of this experiment was due to their above-average teaching abilities. Imagine their shock when it was revealed that they had been picked precisely because of their average abilities. Because of what they had been told, the teachers had a confident expectation in their own abilities and that of their students. This dominant feeling produced a very positive environment, which brought about the best possible results. This is what is known as Confident Expectations or Expectancy Theory and it forms the basis of the Positive Mental Attitude (PMA).

ATTITUDE IS EVERYTHING

A good attitude constitutes 85 per cent of one's success. Attitude, along with two other essentials, determines your likely level of prosperity. Skills, the second essential, are, for example, the ability to repair a car or perform brain surgery. Skills can be learned. The third essential is knowledge. This is what we learn through reading, schooling, attending seminars, etc. You cannot practice a skill without the knowledge of how to apply it. Skills and knowledge combined will equal someone's ability to perform a function. There are a lot of people who are physically and mentally capable of doing a particular job, but for some reason have chosen not to do the job well. That is an issue of attitude.

Think of all the people you know who have been fired from their jobs. Exclude those who lost their jobs because of downsizing or the inability to perform their job because of poor health. Now, ask yourself, were these people fired because they did not know how to do their job, or were they fired because they chose not to do the job well? The latter is most likely. Those people would not have been hired if they did not know how to do the job. At some point, therefore, they must have consciously decided that they were not going to do the job to the best of their ability. In other words, it was their attitude towards their work, not their lack of skills and knowledge, that got them fired. Attitude is the glue that holds our success together.

POSITIVE MENTAL ATTITUDE

One of the easiest formulae to reprogram your subconscious mind for success is called the 21-day PMA (Positive Mental Attitude) Diet. Do not think of the word *diet* in a negative way. A diet involves nothing more than regulating the quantity and quality of something into a system. For example, on a food diet, you are controlling the amount of food (quantity) and the type of food (quality) that goes into your body (system), over a period of time. In the financial sense, we are talking about controlling the quantity and quality of positive thoughts in your mind for 21 days. Why 21 days? Studies show it takes 21 days to form a habit.

Here are the steps you need to take. The first seven days are for identifying the new beliefs, the next seven are for programming the new beliefs and the last seven days are for reinforcing and maintaining the new beliefs.

Physical homework
Set the goal.
Write the goal in bank book.
Place bank book on the fridge.
Review spending habits.
Hide credit cards.

Mental homework
Engage in positive self talk.
Visualize yourself succeeding.

Just carry enough cash for
   what you need.
Stay out of stores.
Frequently deposit dollars
   in bank.

As you can see from the chart we have divided the work into physical and mental tasks. The first physical task is to set the financial goal. Simply by writing it down and placing a deadline on it, you will turn it from a dream into a goal. This exercise involves saving money. You can use a variation of this for almost any goal you choose. For our purposes, the next step is to write the dollar value of your goal on the top of a long page. Underneath it draw a thermometer marked off in ten per cent increments of the goal. Many charities use this tool to show the progress of their fund raising campaigns. Doing this will help you connect to and accept the idea that you will be successful in achieving your goal and encouraging you as you come closer to it. By seeing it, it becomes easier to believe; by believing it, it becomes easier to achieve.

Place the Goal Meter on your refrigerator, or any place that you will see it on a daily basis. Then start to "fill in" the Meter.

> The chains of habit are too light to be felt until they are too heavy to be broken.
>
> – Warren Buffett,
> Investment Billionaire

Review your spending habits. It is one thing to understand your destination, but it is not enough. You have to analyze your present situation and understand what factors have contributed to you being at your present point. By understanding your spending habits you will be able to track the reasons for your lack of surplus cash. We will get into this more in Section B.

Hide your credit cards! If you suffer from impulsive buying, try carrying only enough cash to make your intended purchase when you go to a store. This technique will stop you from picking up that extra bag of chips, magazine or new wrench that you do not really need.

Stay out of stores. You can further resist the temptation of impulse buying by staying out of the stores where you commit the most impulsive buying. Go for a walk in the park instead. You'll be healthier, more relaxed and richer. If you must go to the store, stick to your list and get only what you need. Make frequent deposits in your bank. Even if it is only small amounts. It is important to establish the new habit of depositing money. As you watch your Goal Meter grow, the behavior is reinforced and you'll be rewarded as you see your savings accumulate quite quickly.

Now for the simultaneous mental work. You must engage in positive self-talk. This is where you give yourself constant positive pep talks to encourage you to develop the new attitudes and behaviors. Visualize yourself succeeding. Spend as little as five minutes every day sitting comfortably and imagining yourself succeeding at your goal. This does not only mean picturing yourself with more money in the bank, if that is your current goal, it also involves imagining yourself following the new routines and habits and feeling the exhilarating sense of accomplishment you get when you succeed at something challenging. The degree to which you can plant positive images in your mind will begin to make you comfortable with the physical changes you have made.

Now, some of you may be thinking that this sounds like so much New Age doublespeak and is not worth bothering with. Well, first of all it makes sense. If you fill your body with fattening, unhealthy foods, you should not be surprised when you start to become large and lazy. It is the same principle with your mind and behaviors. Secondly, you would not be reading this book if you were perfectly happy with your economic condition; so your past behaviors have not been entirely effective. Therefore, you have really got nothing to lose.

If you do these visualizations faithfully for 21 days you will start to develop a series of habits that will change your life. Remember, it is like quitting smoking: Do not give into the "cravings" and give up the program or you will be back where you started!

COMFORT ZONES

Comfort zones can really work against you. We have all read examples of minimum-wage workers who have won a fortune from a lottery. They often come from families that are not used to having very much money. Unfortunately, within a matter of years or even months they manage to spend all their winnings. Since they were not accustomed to having much money, the idea of having more money than they could ever imagine throws them entirely out of their financial comfort zone. The burden of being wealthy and the foreignness of it all, becomes so uncomfortable that their only way of dealing with it is to return to a level that is comfortable. They are psychologically programmed, in a way, to misspend their riches until their funds are exhausted. Although they usually feel foolish for squandering their riches, they are actually happier because they have returned to the level at which they are most comfortable. These people have a very serious need to read this book and adjust their attitudes and habits before cashing their winning ticket.

Many well-documented cases of this kind of problem come from the music and entertainment industry. In the many years we have spent interviewing and working with musicians, we have met a large number who, after becoming hugely successful, found themselves in situations they could not handle. Many turned to substance abuse or other destructive habits, even suicide, as ways of dealing with this unaccustomed overnight success. After achieving everything they had worked for and dreamed of, it turned out to be a very empty experience in itself. Fortunately, there are an equal number whose strong sense of self, together with an appreciation of the importance of their families and friends, has resulted in an achievement of real success. So, here is another relevant maxim to consider: Be careful what you wish for, it might just come true. We are not suggesting that you should not have high aspirations and lofty goals, just that you should take these goals one step at a time and understand why you want them, so that you can mentally prepare yourself for success.

One of the ways to adjust to new comfort zones, as we saw in the PMA Diet, is to change your self-talk. In order to program your subconscious mind for success, you have to change the way you talk to yourself on a daily basis. There are two ways to do this: the first is using Positive Affirmation Statements. That is what Denis used to rid himself of the terror of speaking in front of an audience.

You are bombarded with negative signals which reinforce your negative self-concepts. So, you need to turn that around and bombard yourselves with positive signals. Every time you repeat a set of positive affirmations to yourself, you are sending a very strong message to your subconscious mind. You are programming it to accept a new way of thinking about yourself. If you keep doing this over and over again, you reach the point where you have actually changed your subconscious mind's self-concept of your abilities in a given area.

THE POWER OF CREATIVE VISUALIZATION

Once you have been using these Positive Affirmation Statements to create a new comfort zone, the second technique, called Creative Visualization, really brings it all together. Creative Visualization involves taking the time to close your eyes and do a little fantasizing or role-playing. In this, you actually see yourself being very successful in the area you are trying to program into your subconscious. For example, if you are saying to yourself that you want to earn a million dollars, start imagining your new surroundings. Think of the type of house you will live in and where it is located. Make it realistic. Remember that you are not going to get a castle or a mansion overnight. You do not want to be like the hapless lottery winner who ends up losing everything. Keep your visualizations to manageable increments.

> Money isn't everything...but it ranks right up there with oxygen.
>
> – Rita Davenport,
> Motivational Speaker

If you currently live in a house worth $100,000, visualize a house worth $250,000 for the time being. That is in a neighborhood in which you are likely to be comfortable. You can always move up in the future as you make more money and set higher goals for yourself. Wealthy people, as you will learn in Section B of this book, keep their targets realistic and their spending under control. So, imagine a nicer house, the type of school you want your children to attend and how you will fit into this new community. Visualizing this helps you paint a vivid mental picture of yourself being successful and accomplishing this change in your life. You are programming this feeling – this attitude, to become real and solidifying your new comfort zone, whether it is your ideal weight, becoming an accomplished professional, developing more confidence, earning more money or whatever area in which you want to be successful.

If you stay highly focused and keep reciting these Positive Affirmation Statements together with Creative Visualizations for a period of 21 days without stopping, it will create the foundation for real change. If you have passion and energy for this change in your life then, by the end of 21 days, you will have created a brand new comfort zone in which to live. When you combine this with the behaviors, the savings and investment habits and other wealth-building techniques described later in this book you will have what you need to be financially successful.

The following story exemplifies the success that is within your reach when applying these techniques.

Our friend, Anthony, dreamed out loud about owning a flashy BMW Z4. After repeated mentions of this dream, we decided to see if he was serious about this goal. We asked him specifically when he would own the Z4 and how he would gather the necessary funds.

Anthony did not have a date or a plan, just the fantasy. We told him that unless he made several changes, he would never get the car of his dreams. The first step was to set a specific date. The second was to create a savings strategy to obtain the money. These steps were part of the physical homework. What remained was the mental homework.

To assist him in becoming comfortable with the idea of owning the new car we took him to the local BMW dealer, located a new red Z4 and with a digital camera took a picture of Anthony leaning against the car as if he owned it. We took another photo of him driving the car (during the test drive) and another from behind him in the car. We also asked him to close his eyes (after he had parked) and describe the smells of the car – the new car smell, leather upholstery, etc. – and to note the feeling of being in the car. The reason for all this was to give him a multisensory connection with the car. Later, back in Anthony's home, we printed and placed the pictures in prominent spots such as the refrigerator, the bathroom mirror and inside his daily planner as positive reminders. The idea was for him to use the visuals as constant reminders of his goal. The more he saw himself in the car the more accustomed his mind would become to the idea.

Anthony reviewed his financial situation and determined that he needed to save a lot of money for the down payment of the car. As a result he decided to apply for that better paying job that he had been procrastinating about for several weeks. He got the job and the pay increase but, most importantly, vowed not to increase his life-style. Instead, he cut his costs. He consolidated his debt by getting rid of his high interest credit cards and took out a small loan that he paid off over 12 months. The loan was for $10,000 at 7.5 per cent and he placed this money in a bank savings certificate at five per cent. Obviously this strategy cost him $250 but it became a forced savings plan. He had to repay the loan so he got used to having the payment automatically deducted every month.

In another strategy he took his weekly spending money of $125 as cash at the beginning of each week and placed it into his right pocket. Every time he went to make a purchase he would look at the picture in his daytimer and ask himself if it was really necessary. More often than not he would decide against the purchase and transfer that amount over to his left pocket. At the end of the week he would take the money from his left pocket and put it into his savings account. Any money remaining in his right pocket would go towards the next week's fund.

Following these simple strategies, Anthony saved $12,823 over the 12-month period ($2,823 plus the $10,000 loan). The lease on his old car expired the day before he was to purchase his Z4. That afternoon he used the $12,823 as the downpayment and financed the balance over a three-year period. With this healthy downpayment, his monthly loan was $100 less than his previous lease payment. He took this $100 monthly surplus and rewarded himself by opening an IRA. Today, after applying these and other creative savings habits (many of which are outlined in later chapters), he owns a beautiful, mortgage-free condo overlooking the ocean and still maximizes his annual IRA contribution. He was able to accomplish all of this through visualizations and a simple, but very effective, realignment in his normal spending and savings habits.

There is nothing Anthony did that you could not do with the same expectation of success. To prepare yourself for victory, you need to apply this approach to changes you want to make in your personal and business life, knowing that if you put effort into it, you are going to be successful. There are more strategies like this available on our website, www.abcguys.com; click on our VIP Coaching services.

BLAME VS RESPONSIBILITY

It is really easy to blame others for your financial problems. If someone else is at fault then you can avoid taking any action indefinitely. Blaming others looks to the past. Taking responsibility looks to the future. The only part of your history you can control is the present and the way you can control it is to take responsibility for your financial situation. How do you stop blaming other people for your own shortcomings? The ability to make any change begins with awareness. The very fact that you took the action of getting and reading this book increases your awareness significantly.

Try this brief exercise:

1. Make a list of things you think you should do and another list of things you should not do. For example, "I should be better prepared and organized at work" or "I should not get angry with my co-workers."

   _____   _____

   _____   _____

   _____   _____

2. Now, change "I should" to "I will" and "I should not" to "I will not", whichever is appropriate.

   _____   _____

   _____   _____

   _____   _____

Examine the different feelings you experience as you say both phrases. You will probably feel more powerful when you change "I should" to "I will" or "I should not" to "I will not". When you take responsibility for your actions you have much more power. You are then able to take control of your life.

Blaming banks for high interest rates on credit cards will get you nowhere. A much more productive step would be to take responsibility for your credit problems, pay off the balance and cut up the cards. You will save a bundle on interest charges and can invest that money in an investment plan. Blaming someone else for not advancing in your company will also get you nowhere. Take responsibility for yourself and come up with a new plan. Take some courses, for example, so that your boss cannot deny your advancement or use the extra training to get a better job at another company.

A lot of people who do not succeed in life know all the reasons for their lack of achievement. A character analyst (unknown name) compiled a list of the most commonly used alibis. As you read this list, examine yourself carefully and determine how many of these alibis, if any, are in your own vocabulary.

I would be more successful...

IF I did not have a spouse and a family.

IF I had enough "pull."

IF I had money.

IF I had a good education.

IF I could get a job.

IF I had good health.

IF I only had time.

IF times were better.

IF other people understood me.

IF conditions around me were only different.

IF I could live my life over again.

IF I did not fear what "they" would say.

IF I had been given a chance.

IF other people did not "have it in for me."

IF nothing happens to stop me.

IF I were only younger.

IF I could only do what I want.

IF I had been born rich.

IF I could meet the right people.

IF I had the talent some people have.

IF I dared assert myself.

IF I had only embraced past opportunities.

IF people did not get on my nerves.

IF I did not have to keep the house and look after the kids.

IF I could save some money.

IF the boss only appreciated me.

IF I only had someone to help me.

IF my family understood me.

IF I lived in a big city.

IF I could just get started.

IF I were only free.

IF I had the personality of some people.

IF I were not so overweight.

IF my talents were known.

IF I could just get a break.

IF I could only get out of debt.

IF I had not failed.

IF I only knew how.

IF everyone did not oppose me.

IF I did not have so many worries.

IF I could marry the right person.

IF people were not so stupid.

IF my family were not so extravagant.

IF I were sure of myself.

IF luck were not against me.

IF I had not been born under the wrong star.

IF it were not true that "what is to be will be."

IF I did not have to work so hard.

IF I had not lost my money.

IF I lived in a different neighborhood.

IF I did not have a "past."

IF I only had a business of my own.

IF other people would only listen to me.

If you have read and understood this chapter and are prepared to make the necessary changes, then you will realize that every one of these alibis is now obsolete. Here is the toughest one of all. When you can say this without wincing you will be taking responsibility for yourself and your actions and ready to accomplish almost anything, which includes becoming wealthier: If I have the courage to see myself as I really am, I will analyze my shortcomings and correct them. Then I will have a chance to profit from my mistakes and be open to learning new things.

Just to make sure that you are ready to move on to the next step, let's review what we have discussed in this chapter.

1. What were my original beliefs about wealth?
2. Who put these opinions in my mind?
3. Do these thoughts need to be altered?
4. What is my new definition of wealth?
5. Why are some people more successful than others?
6. What is my Personal Life Mission Statement?
7. What is my Personal Definition of Success?
8. What are the financial situations I fear the most?

9. Am I prepared to change these fears into anticipated events?
10. Do I blame other people for my shortcomings?
11. What is my action plan for getting the things that I want?
12. Are the things that I visualize realistic and achievable?
13. What are my Positive Affirmation Statements?
14. Describe my visualization of success.

When you have an answer to each and every one of these questions, then and only then will you be fully ready to move on to the next chapter. Please take your time with these questions. Some of the answers may be difficult for you. The more difficult they are, the greater your need to answer them. At the risk of sounding preachy or condescending, we want to make it clear that by circumventing this process you are short-changing your financial future. If you are willing to do this work, the other steps will flow easily and your wealth will increase exponentially.

> By the time they have made it, most people forget what "it" was.
>
> – Malcolm Forbes

In the next chapter, Powerful Attitudes for Becoming a Money Magnet, you will be taking these ideas one step further by contrasting two very different types of people: the Money Minimizer and the Money Magnet. You will learn three critical points that will assist you in your fast track to making money.

POWERFUL ATTITUDES FOR BECOMING A MONEY MAGNET

Congratulations! Making it to Chapter 2 indicates that you have commitment and a real desire to change even deeply held attitudes. This means that you are already well on the way to a positive financial change. Don't worry, we will soon be getting to the specific tips for making and saving money. First though, we want you to consider a few more adjustments to the way you think about money that will pay huge dividends once you start to accumulate it in greater amounts.

In this chapter we are going to look at how to adopt or change your attitudes so that they are consistent with those of the wealthy. Simply put, when you learn to think like a millionaire it is much easier to become one.

In our experience and through our research, we have found that the world is generally divided into two camps. 90 per cent are Money Minimizers while the other ten per cent are Money Magnets. The fundamental difference between the two is that their attitudes toward money are very different.

The Money Minimizer's primary attitude regarding money is that in order to be successful he or she must work for money. This implies getting the best job, one that is very secure, paying the highest salary, with the best benefits, learning more and working harder to get the next promotion, etc. The Money Magnet, on the other hand, believes that in order to be successful, money has to work for them. Ten per cent get it, 90 per cent pay it.

After decades of studying wealthy people, we have found that they as a group are, not surprisingly, consistently oriented towards wealth accumulation. Now, with some, this becomes an all-encompassing compulsion and although they may be very happy, they might also be missing out on other pleasures of life. Our thinking is that there is a time and place for everything and that everything needs to be in balance. We are not advocating the adoption of wealth accumulation as your new religion; what we are suggesting is that you take the most powerful elements of this attitude and include them in your new way of thinking. We call this becoming a Money Magnet.

When you ask most people if they wish to become wealthy they usually respond in the positive. Beyond that, however, they do not really give it much thought. So, the first thing we want to do is to bring this goal out of the background and put it up front where we can see and deal with it. Money is like a magnet in that it has power. That power can be positive or negative. If you do not understand money then it will control you; you will become a slave to it. Once you understand that money has power and you start to gain control of it, you can harness it and turn it into a positive for yourself – have it work for you.

One of the reasons people find it hard to harness the power of money is, as we discussed in Chapter 1, that they fear it. For example, the fear of losing our apartment or home keeps us working diligently at a job. The only difference between working as a secretary in an office, a worker on an assembly line or as an engineer or lab technician is the life-style one can afford. In each circumstance they may all be working as a slave to their pay checks and the life-style they have selected. They cannot step back and enjoy what they have because they are living so close to the edge that if they lose their income for even a few weeks, it would all disappear. That fear is a powerful motivational force and it keeps people tethered to the S.S. Ship of J.O.B. (Just Out of Bankruptcy).

Contrast that with the person who works under the same job description but who has set up a regular investment savings plan, has stopped wasting money on things that they do not really have the time to enjoy anyway, or who has started up another source of income from a part time business. These people are Money Magnets and the main difference is their attitude to money.

A Money Magnet is an individual whose fundamental attitude is that he or she controls money and that money works for them. As we said in Chapter 1, our outer reality is always consistent with our inner reality. Money Magnets intuitively understand the following laws:

- The law of cause and effect. It states that every action has a corresponding and predictable reaction. Therefore, anyone who focuses on wealth-limiting thoughts or those of scarcity, cannot create abundance. The Money Magnet concentrates on the thought that he or she controls money, not the other way around. This will eventually become his or her reality. The Money Magnet saves first and spends what's left over, while the Money Minimizer spends first and saves only if there is anything left over (and there usually isn't).

- The law of the Golden Chalice. This says, to use the old cliche, the glass can be half full or half empty. A surprising number of people choose to see the glass as half empty. When the stock market is down, the Money Magnet sees the opportunity to purchase stocks at a discount. When a Money Magnet sees a business that is beating everyone's expectations, he or she sells their stake and reaps the profit before any unforeseen circumstance creeps in to steal future profits.

- The law of lifetime learning. Learning equals earning. There is a distinct correlation between learning and wealth generation. If you are not growing as an individual through learning then the financial part of you is dying. The Money Magnet is naturally curious and eager to learn about how businesses function, how tax laws can be made to work in their favor and how investments work, to name a few. By investing time in a general knowledge of money matters, he or she will see opportunities and be better equipped to qualify them when they are presented. You probably already know plenty of poor people, it is time now to get to know the wealthy. If you want to be wealthy, hang out with wealthy people.

WHY MOST PEOPLE BECOME MONEY MINIMIZERS

People often ask us to explain how the Money Minimizer mindset became so pervasive. It is a difficult question. At the risk of making sweeping generalizations, the school system, formal religions and the home unit have all been key historical "environmental" forces shaping how today's children think about money and related financial issues.

The mandate of the average school system is to prepare a large group of children to function in the society. Children, however, have different needs and learn at their own pace. Unfortunately, most school systems are not geared towards the individual and are forced to go for the average. Independence gets lost in the shuffle and replaced with mantras like: following the rules, working very hard, getting good grades, going to a trade school or university, getting a job, being a good worker, listening obediently to the boss in order to get a promotion and eventually retiring with a pension. Another casualty of most public schools is that young people are not taught how to budget, invest money or start their own businesses. Some formal religions and governments are similarly geared towards the masses and not the encouragement of the individual. All of these factors result in a Money Minimizing mindset that gets passed on from generation to generation.

Traditionally, the wealthy, or as we like to call them Money Magnets, for the most part go to private schools where money management, outside-of-the-box thinking and entrepreneurialism is part of the curriculum. These students have the opportunity to interact with peers coming from similar families and backgrounds. Their teachers and parents expect them to be the leaders of tomorrow. The schools are very well resourced and have low student/teacher ratios. In short everyone, including the student, has a confident expectation that the child will be successful or wealthy and thus it is no surprise that the vast majority realize their potential. Think of the example from Chapter 1 illustrating the power of the teacher's expectations on a student's performance. In short, Money Magnets get richer while Money Minimizers work all of their lives just to keep their heads above the financial waters, anchoring themselves to the vessel called the S.S. J.O.B.

The difference in orientation between the families of Money Minimizers and Money Magnets is that one will encourage their children to work for a good company, while the other encourages them to own a good company. Young Money Magnets in the making, sitting at the family supper table, do not hear messages of scarcity. They are brought up overhearing their parents discussing abundance, the acquisitions of companies, investment strategies, methods for reducing taxes and creative business opportunities. These wealth creation ideas become some of the dominant thoughts in the young persons' minds. These thoughts eventually manifest themselves as real wealth.

Poor families talk about financial pain and scarcity or they do not talk about money at all in front of their children. Wealthy families believe that a young child's financial education starts at home. The scarcity thinking of a Money Minimizer is the result of fear. The fear of losing a job, the fear that the price of gas will increase, the fear that the landlord will increase the rent, or the fear that the car will not last another season. Scarcity thinking results in short-term, reactionary and victim behaviors rather than proactive, long-term, victor behaviors that are the hallmark of Money Magnets. The first requirement for the emerging Money Magnet therefore, is to discard any old attitudes that would jeopardize their money making plans and develop the necessary wealth creation behaviors, which incidentally is the focus of Chapters 3 to 7.

Here is a story about a guy who avoids that kind of limiting thinking. Denis was travelling through Singapore in 1995 on a speaking engagement. While out for some exercise with Graham, a British colleague, they walked along Orchard Road – the Rodeo Drive of Singapore.

"Pausing in front of an electronic store we met a short, stocky, engaging man named Steven who was full of fun and enthusiasm. Unlike all of his neighbors, he was standing on the street in front of the store in which he worked and had a warm greeting and a joke for everyone walking by, whether they showed any interest in his store or not. We engaged in the usual tourist banter including options for getting out of the city to experience some of the unique natural phenomenon of the island nation. Steven suggested we visit the famous Night Safari Zoo that explodes with nocturnal animal life every evening. When Graham lamented leaving his camera at home, Steven suggested he had the perfect answer in a reasonably low cost point-and-shoot camera that, with the right film and some of his night shooting tips, would take memorable pictures. Captivated by his relentless energy and enthusiasm Graham bought the camera and was not disappointed in the promised quality.

"Six months later, on a return engagement, I went for another walk and found a much different atmosphere. It was just past the height of the Asian Economic Crisis. Pessimism pervaded most people's thinking. Many businesses had closed, most had laid off staff and the rest were waiting expectantly for their seemingly inevitable end. Turning to Orchard Road, the carnage had one bright spot. Steven was in his customary position bounding with new energy. A month earlier his boss had decided to cut his losses and abandon the shop before he was forced to shut it down. Steven had a different attitude. He asked for advice from some of the well-off customers that he knew, then took most of the money he had been saving over the past 15 years, paid his boss a fire sale price for the business and assumed the lease.

"Steven reasoned that his country's currency crisis was a golden buying opportunity for visitors from certain other nations and started to cater to American and British tourists. He had a big banner installed which showed a set of scales with a huge US dollar weighing down one end and the currencies of all the Asian nations swinging up in the breeze. He had a flyer printed up outlining the 50 'not to be missed' photographic locations in Singapore, courtesy of Steven's Cameras and Electronics, and had it distributed to every four and five-star hotel in the area. He had also taken to reading American and British newspapers in order to better engage his visitors as he spoke about sports teams and current events. Seeing all this, I asked Steven about his apparent success. Steven's reply was simple, yet very powerful 'You need to be aware of the economy, but not preoccupied by it. Doom and gloom is good for selling newspapers and robbing people of their sleep. It can also hide opportunities. The average person has little or no control over the economy but they can control their personal economy if they choose to. I saw an opportunity and was prepared to make the necessary personal and business investments to guarantee my success.'"

To our way of thinking Steven is a Money Magnet who has, through his attitude, independent perspective and commitment to learning, tapped into the power of magnetism.

Think of a rich and successful person as a powerful magnet and yourself, at this point, like a paperclip in one of those paper clip dispensers. A paperclip is not magnetic but after being held by the magnet for a while, it picks up some of the charge and can actually attract other paperclips to itself. The greater the magnetic force and the longer the exposure, the greater the energizing effect. In the human context the same phenomenon holds true. We see it on a regular basis when people leave our seminars. You have probably seen it after your company's annual sales convention. People are charged up and more effective at whatever they've been studying for a period of time before the charge wears off. Your charge needs to be constantly re-energized, so you do not lose momentum. By associating with and learning from wealthy people the average person begins to think and act in a similar fashion thus increasing his own wealth-generating abilities. Think of a tennis match. If you play with someone worse than yourself, it is hard to improve your game. When you play with someone better, you push yourself and your game improves. The key to developing and maintaining long-term Money Magnetism is to associate with and start to think and act like Money Magnets.

> Rule One. You must know the difference between an asset and a liability and buy assets. Poor and middle-class people acquire liabilities which they think are assets. An asset is something that puts money in my pocket. A liability is something that takes money out of my pocket.
>
> – Robert T. Kiyoski,
> Author of *Rich Dad, Poor Dad*

As in any sport it is good to know how you rank as a player. Here is a quick summary of the principles in this chapter, which will help rank your effective attraction to money.

Step 1: Are you comfortable with and convinced of the idea that money works for you and you control it, rather than the opposite scenario?

Step 2: If you had a positive answer to Step 1 then you are well on your way to fully developing your Money Magnetism potential. If you are still questioning this concept then you have to resolve it or it will become the barrier that keeps you from becoming wealthy. If you need to, go back to Chapter 1 and determine who or what in your past is keeping you anchored to these limiting beliefs.

Step 3: Examine the way you are currently living your life and ask yourself if you are being consistent with the three laws of being a Money Magnet. If you are not fully living all three of the laws then you are not utilizing your full potential and need to focus on the weak area(s).

The following questions will help to ensure that you get the best "returns" from this chapter:

1. What is the difference between a Money Minimizer and a Money Magnet?
2. How is it in my best interest to become a Money Magnet?

3. What specific Money Minimizer attitudes must I drop in order to move forward financially?
4. What specific Money Magnet attitudes do I need to adopt in order to reach my goals?
5. How can I use the three Money Magnet Laws to create wealth?
6. Which Money Magnets do I currently know that I need to spend more time with?
7. Which Money Magnets do I need to meet in the near future?
8. What is my plan to meet and associate with these Money Magnets?
9. Why would these people want to associate with me?
10. Am I fully convinced that from this point on money works for me and I am committed to developing the necessary behaviors to create extraordinary wealth?

We are now at the end of the first section. In many ways this can be the most difficult part of the process because we are dealing with attitudes that you may have been living with since you were very young. If you have adopted these new principles, then we congratulate you. You are way ahead of most of your neighbors and about to move into a newer, richer phase of your life.

The next section deals with specific behaviors for wealth generation that are relatively simple to implement assuming you have already adjusted your attitude. If adapting these behaviors is problematic then you need to go back and review the first two chapters. In order to become really successful you have to get through Section A – Attitudes before you go on to Section B – Behaviors and subsequently, you have to get through that successfully before you take on Section C – Creation.

As an illustration of this, after about a week at a resort writing and watching people frolicking and having fun in the pool we noticed a man who never seemed to go near the water. In passing, one afternoon, we asked him if he was "allergic" to pools. After a bit of joking he confided his deep and abiding fear of water. We had seen him earlier actively participating in a game of beach volleyball. So we knew that he was physically able to walk to the pool, hold his breath and jump into the water. Therefore, he could easily strap on a life vest and adapt the necessary mechanics to go to the pool. He just couldn't make himself get into the water. As a father he would watch his children swim and could offer constructive criticism on their techniques. This is the difference between *knowing* and *being*. *Knowing* – having the learning – plus *doing* the appropriate actions equals *being*. This man knew the techniques of swimming just like you may now be able to recognize a Money Magnet and describe the attributes of one. The question is: Can you be one, or in other words, can you jump into the water?

All the knowledge in the world couldn't make this man do so. Reading all the financial books in the world cannot make you rich if you are not able to mentally make the jump. For most people, getting into a pool is as simple as it is enjoyable. Most do not think about it, we just do it. For some people, saving and making money is a natural activity. But for most people it is not second nature and that is why we have spent so much time emphasizing the importance of this step. If you are really ready to *be* wealthy, then adapting the behaviors outlined in the next few chapters will be easy and soon become second nature. If they are not, then you may need to relearn how to swim.

SECTION II

———— ✦ ————

BEHAVIORS FOR MAKING MONEY

3

THE BEHAVIORS OF GOAL ACHIEVERS

You may have heard the expression: If it looks like a duck, acts like a duck and quacks like a duck, chances are it is not an eagle, it is a duck. If the duck wants to hang out with the eagles, then it is going to have to find a way to fit in. It is the same with being rich. If you want to become wealthy then you have to be comfortable in the environment of rich people and in turn they have to be comfortable with you. In other words, if you want to go to a formal reception, showing up in ripped jeans and a T-shirt is not going to help you fit in or gain acceptance. A tourist who spends a week in an all-inclusive resort in a Caribbean country may think that he or she knows the reality of that culture, but they would be wrong. To understand that environment requires leaving the property and mingling with the locals. If you want to be accepted by the local population, first you will have to leave the comfort zone of the resort. Then you have to be open to seeing the new reality. Trying to impose your value system on them will not encourage them to open up to you. The more you can open yourself up and blend in with them, the more likely they are to really open up to you. It is the same with wealthy people. They are more likely to share tax-savings plans and wealth-generating ideas among people with whom they feel comfortable.

Here is an example. Recently, Denis was invited to attend a gala fund-raising event featuring former President Bill Clinton as guest speaker. It was a major social event, attracting several blue chip sponsors and hundreds of people representing all facets of the societal elite. Supporters of the children's charity could attend the dinner and speech at a cost of $350 per person, or for $1,000 attend the dinner and a private reception with Mr. Clinton.

"When I entered the Grand Ballroom I met a busy man in his late forties who was running around directing people to their appropriate places. His name was Manuel, who, I later learned, was an independent Realtor for 16 years catering to the mid-range home market. Though successful he was finding it very difficult to move into the upscale home market where his real passion lay. When he first heard about the event and thought about the type of upscale audience it would attract he began to think of ways to connect with this wealthy group. He could pay the $350 admission fee, but feared that he wouldn't fit in with the upscale guests.

"He decided to approach the management company organizing the evening and offer his services as a volunteer. His first assignment was to approach the secondary media for free public service coverage of the event as the main newspapers, radio and television stations were already signed up as media sponsors. Drawing on his previous experience in selling to various ethnic markets, Manuel contacted and sold some key decision-makers on the event's newsworthiness with Mr. Clinton coming to town and the fact that an important local charity was the beneficiary. Over several months Manuel personally met and developed relationships with over a dozen independent media owners. The organizers were very pleased with his results and in turn invited him to assist the team on the night of the event.

"His primary role was to greet guests as they arrived, direct them to the appropriate registration area and then help them find their reserved seats. Manuel was then free to join everyone else in the pre-dinner networking. At dinner he had the opportunity to sit across the table from a wealthy couple who had been having trouble finding an available, larger house on the water. Remembering a conversation with the successful owner of an independent ethnic newspaper in the region, who as a recent empty nester was looking to downsize, he suggested that he might be able to help them. When he described the house, the couple gave him their phone number and made him promise to call them the next day. Manuel planned to approach the publisher for a viewing and, as a deal sweetener, offer to exchange part of his fees for free advertising space in his newspaper, thereby gaining promotion and credibility in that ethnic market. We never heard how it turned out but Manuel does get a gold star for creativity and initiative."

"My three colleagues and I sat at a table with, a Vice-president of sales, a venture capitalist, a couple that owned an international import–export business and a young single woman named Claire. Claire and I talked about current events, various children's issues and the positive impact that this event would have on the local charity. I was impressed that a person so young would demonstrate the maturity and wisdom normally associated with someone ten years her senior. I was quite surprised to learn later in the conversation that she was a full-time student. Intrigued, I wanted to learn what prompted a student to spend $350 to attend that type of event. She told me that she learned of the gala fund-raiser from her local community newspaper and thought the evening would be a wonderful way to hear a live presentation of President Clinton, a man she had respected for many years. It also provided the opportunity for her to meet many influential people while helping a local cause that she deeply believed in. She also admitted that coming up with the $350 out of her limited student budget was a real financial stretch for her.

"She was in her last year of a childcare studies degree. Her dream was to start her own consulting business implementing the model she had developed to set up "turn key" corporate daycare centres. The idea being that the daycare centre would act as a staff retention or motivational tool while providing a solid, safe, caring and learning environment for the children. I asked her what she would consider a successful outcome for the evening. She replied that she wanted to expand her understanding of how powerful, wealthy people acted, thought, networked and socialized. She also wanted their views on daycare. She shared the fact that the room did intimidate her and part of her felt that she was in over her head.

"Moments later, out of the corner of my eye, I spotted a previous client who was the director of Human Resources for a successful local company. I waved him over. We exchanged quick pleasantries and I introduced him to Claire. A brief conversation ensued and a future meeting was arranged for a more detailed presentation. After he left, she turned to me and said, 'You set me up, I was not even slightly prepared to talk to that guy.' I replied 'I thought that you handled yourself very well and you made a compelling argument for your model. You may not have been prepared to the extent that you wanted to be, however, when an opportunity arises you have to be prepared to seize the moment. Remember this slogan when embarking on a new set of behaviors: 'Sometimes you have to fake it till you make it.'"

> If you are not recreating yourself constantly, you are probably not going to be accommodating the reality of your world.
>
> – William G. McGowan,
> Founder and Chairman, MCI

This story is an illustration of Reality Immersion. That is a technique used when a person puts him or herself in a situation or an environment that they wish to understand better. In the example above, both Claire and Manuel associated with wealthy people with the aim of learning more about them, being more comfortable in dealing with them and to ultimately become wealthy themselves. They both had specific goals in mind and the fund-raising event was a means to learn while moving towards their goal. They are both Money Magnets that came up with creative ways to be part of an environment rich in opportunities for personal and business growth.

Another example of Reality Immersion is a bookstore owner who notices that someone is stealing his books. He tries various methods to reduce theft including the installation of electronic barriers, signs noting that shoplifters will be prosecuted, doing integrity checks on his staff and instituting a policy of having all shopping bags checked at the security counter. Despite these measures he is still losing books. He then uses the Reality Immersion technique to solve his problem by hiring a professional shoplifter as a consultant. The shoplifter takes the bookstore owner on a tour of the bookshop and describes every point that is vulnerable to theft. In this example the shop owner has overcome his problem of theft by learning to think like a shoplifter. This technique, not the shoplifting, applies to becoming wealthier. One of the first steps in becoming wealthy is understanding how rich people think and act.

Before proceeding any further we need to point out that Reality Immersion should never involve trying to take advantage of another person, or to place the burden and responsibility of your success on someone else's shoulders. The principle behind this technique is to learn from rather than take from the rich. This is not a modern day psychological Robin Hood approach of the poor robbing the rich! In it is truest form, both parties are enriched by the experience.

THE BENEFITS OF ASSOCIATING WITH WEALTHY PEOPLE

We have a seminar and television show devoted to building self-esteem in teenagers. In it there is a slogan that says, "If your friends and associates are negative people, do not walk away from them, RUN!" In suggesting that you start to associate closer with wealthy and successful people, we are not saying that you should start to use people. The idea is that you are more likely to push yourself on to greater wealth accumulation if you are associating with rich people than if you are hanging around poor people.

Do not forget to keep things in perspective. Some wealthy people live only to accumulate more money. They may be able

to aid you in your quest for greater wealth. On the other hand, some of your poorer friends may have avoided the pursuit of the dollar in favor of stronger family and community values. We believe that true happiness combines all perspectives.

The first step in associating with wealthy people is to identify which type of wealthy people you wish to associate with. Once this is determined, you should make a point to try and connect with them. On the surface, wealthy people may seem distant, aloof or guarded when it comes to being approached by strangers. The reason for this behavior is it acts as a protective shield to keep people from trying to take advantage of them and their wealth. Over the years we have asked our wealthy friends and clients what subjects Money Minimizers approach them about and the answer has always been the same: "They want me to buy something from them, lend them some money or give them a job." They all report that virtually no one has ever asked them how they became rich; nor has anyone asked them to share their most valuable asset – their knowledge.

We have made a point over the years to get to know wealthy people and their stories. As these relationships develop, a sense of trust is formed. When they realize that all we want is their friendship and to understand some of what they have learned, they are very happy to open up. In short, most people are interested only in a wealthy person's money; the difference is we are interested in learning *how* they made their money.

> The shortest and best way to make your fortune is to let people see clearly that it is in their interests to promote yours.
>
> – Jean de La bruyere

If you are going to start associating more closely with wealthy people, you need to learn the language of wealth. Here are some suggestions.

Reading Makes You Rich

The value of reading business books and other sources of information is that it will help you to learn and understand what wealthy people think, eat and breathe. Huge amounts of this information are distilled and available to you for free or at a very low cost. The cost of several hours of your time, the cover price of a book, the cost of a public library card and not to mention the unlimited information available on the internet will provide you with an abundance of wealth-building ideas. Try committing to reading a minimum of 30 minutes a day, five days a week. (If you are feeling stretched for time, try watching one less hour of television per day.) This translates, at an average reading speed, to twelve books per year. If you consider that the average adult reads less than one nonfiction book per year, you can plainly see how quickly you will gain an information advantage over the majority of the population.

Read the Business Sections of the Newspapers that are Read by Wealthy People

The Wall Street Journal, New York Times, LA Times, The Economist, The Asian Wall Street Journal or *The Financial Times*. If these newspapers are difficult to find in your community or you do not connect with the style of writing, you can always start by reading the financial or business section of your local newspaper.

Here is a list of URLs for websites providing a treasure trove of free financial information. They range from the pragmatic and easy-to-read to very comprehensive and sophisticated.

www.coolfreebielinks.com
www.servercc.oakton.edu/~wittman/find/finance.htm
www.stock.com
www.net1000.net
www.standard&poor.com
www.scholarstuff.com
www.hoovers.com
www.globeinvestor.com

www.imoney.com
www.investorhome.com
www.sedar.com
www.stockpoint.com

Books you may find useful are listed in Appendix 1 of this book.

Attending Wealth-building Seminars and Workshops

This is another method of learning quickly from someone else's expertise and offers the unique advantage of being able to ask the seminar leader specific questions tailored to your needs. The second advantage is the live element that generates a positive, action inspiring energy within the audience. The third advantage, and in many cases the most significant, is the fact that there are numerous like-minded attendees, which facilitates peer-to-peer networking.

Join Clubs or Professional Associations

These clubs are forums for like-minded people to come together to exchange ideas and receive mentorship from experts.

Consider Enrolling in "Black Tar University"

Countless commuters spend wasted hours getting to and from work. Why not let a financial audiobook (some are available at no cost from libraries or on the web) keep you company in the car or on the train. CDs, podcasts, mp3s and webinars are available to provide you with an opportunity to learn about wealth generating while you commute.

Create Your Own Wealth-building Mastermind Team

This is a mutually beneficial group of like-minded people who choose to come together on a regular basis to exchange information, ideas and strategies to help one another reach their financial goals. This group can comprise the following people: Friends, relatives, neighbors, coworkers, etc. The key point to remember is that each person must be 100 per cent committed to attaining his personal goals and be fully supportive of the rest of the team.

Consider the Concept of Together We Learn and Earn

Each week on a rotational basis, one person in a group, like a mastermind team, takes the lead in presenting to the group some aspect of wealth building that he or she has investigated. It could be a book they have read, a seminar attended or a considered response to any relevant question on which the group has sought more information. The more time and energy the person is prepared to devote to his or her topic, the more they and the group will achieve.

GOAL SETTING

The Link Between Goal Setting and Achieving Wealth

Apart from those people that are, as they say, "currently between opportunities," most people are busier than ever. Despite all the new technological marvels designed to save us time and make us more efficient, everyone we know has less time on their hands than ever before. We seem to be running at breakneck speed from the moment we get up until we hit the pillow 18 hours later. We, as a society, are chronically sleep deprived and experiencing higher levels of stress. Diseases of the heart and other organs are on the rise and relationships suffer. Even children are exhibiting these signs as they are shuttled back and forth between parents and to various extracurricular activities. There is very little room for down time. So, are we any better off? Most people would have to answer negatively and might even say that they are worse off than they were ten years ago. In short, we are doing much more and achieving much less.

Wealthy people understand that being active is not enough. They realize that the key lies in being more productive. They do not work harder; they are just smarter and more productive in what they choose to spend their time on. One of the key characteristics of wealthy people is that they know what they want out of life and know what it will take to get there.

As we said in Chapter 1, you cannot hit a target you cannot see. There is a huge difference between simply wanting more money and taking the necessary steps to design and follow a plan to achieve that goal. That is not to say that most people are bereft of any goals, it's just that those goals do not hit high enough. Generally, people limit their goals to maintaining their current jobs, receiving a small raise at the end of the year or a promotion the next time a job opens up. There is nothing wrong with those goals; it is just that you could do better. The other problem with those particular goals is that they lock people in to the basically flawed structure wherein they are working for someone else. All that the raise or elevated position will do for you is make the treadmill turn more quickly.

It is not that people do not know how to set goals; virtually everyone has in the past set and achieved many goals. Everyone has wanted to buy a car, a special set of clothes, get a certain job or meet a mate. And they have achieved those goals. Now what we are suggesting is that we raise the bar a bit and fine tune what we are all after. You cannot enjoy The Gold if your goals are made of Bronze or Tin.

Why Set Wealth Goals? What's in It for You?

1. It forces you to focus on the specific actions necessary to bring your wealth targets to fruition.
2. It helps identify any weaknesses that need to be resolved before you can achieve success.
3. It converts wishful thinking into reality.
4. It holds you accountable for your own success.
5. When opportunities present themselves, you are better equipped to recognize their value and capitalise on them.
6. It helps you organize the daily activities that will give you the maximum benefit.
7. It increases your odds of actually achieving the goal.

If Setting Wealth Goals is a Primary Key to Success, Why Do So Few People Set Them?

There are four common reasons why most people do not set wealth goals. The first is that people do not realize the awesome power of goal setting as it translates into wealth creation. Secondly, most people do not know how to effectively set wealth goals. After all, this is not something that is taught in most schools. The result is that the majority of people fumble awkwardly through the foreign process of wealth-goal setting with marginal, if any, success.

The third reason is that people are afraid of receiving criticism and rejection from those whom they care about. Often, the emerging Money Magnet will set a challenging wealth goal and share it with a family member or a friend, only to have that other person demoralize them by saying things like: "You can't do that," "Who do you think you are, can't you be grateful for what you have?" This other person is not necessarily trying to harm you but the reality is that their financial comfort zone clashes with your goal so they articulate their discomfort by criticizing or rejecting your goal. If this happens to you, please realize that this is their problem, not yours. It becomes your problem only if you buy into their beliefs.

The final reason is also the most common and the deadliest of the four. It is that people fear failure and disappointment. The fear of failure is the most pervasive reason why people do not set goals. It has debilitated countless millions from living and enjoying the life-style they crave and desire. This fear of failure is often referred to as the "what-if" syndrome.

Meaningful goals can be challenging to set and all the more satisfying when completed. Goals must be S.M.A.R.T. which means: Specific, Measurable, Attainable, Realistic and Timely.

For example, several years ago Alan met Debbie in England. "She was working as support staff in an office. She loved fashion though she could rarely afford to indulge her tastes. She recognized that one of the things holding back any career advancement was that she could not afford to dress in the power suits of her bosses. Deciding to address both issues, she set herself the goal of acquiring a new wardrobe within one year.

She happily did the research and made a list of four outfits that she could mix, match and accessorize to result effectively in seven different looks. The cost would be around $2,500.

"She found a great little boutique that had the best selection for her needs and considered setting up a layaway plan to help her formalise her savings. While chatting with the owner, Debbie learned that the boutique owner was looking for someone to do some needed office work. Not one to miss an opportunity, Debbie suggested a deal which would help both parties. Debbie would work weekends at the store doing what she considered easy tasks. In lieu of payment she would pay down the cost of her clothes on which, as an employee, she would get at a 30 per cent discount. Her creative twist allowed her to meet her goal in about half the time and as a bonus she was able to devote the funds originally designated for the clothes to a savings plan."

Debbie's goal fit all of the criteria of the S.M.A.R.T test, which is part of the reason she was successful.

The Eight Steps to Goal Setting

1. State the money making or wealth creation goal in S.M.A.R.T. terms.
2. Set a deadline for when you plan to achieve it.
3. Analyze your current point relative to your goal.
4. Identify *why* you want to achieve the goal and *how* you will benefit.
5. Identify the obstacles and challenges that you will have to overcome.
6. Identify the people whose help you will need.
7. Identify the knowledge and skills you will have to acquire or further develop.
8. Commit to an action plan with daily, weekly and monthly reminders.

To help yourself, use visualizations and affirmations. Remember, be persistent and do not give up. Learn from your setbacks. Stay focused and positive. Be disciplined.

The following worksheet is called the Wealth Creation Goal Sheet. We suggest you do not write directly in the book but use it as a master for photocopying purposes. A new photocopy should be used for the setting and achieving of each separate goal.

Wealth Creation Goal Sheet

The specific money making or wealth creation goal I will achieve is...

I will achieve this goal by the following date...

My current status/situation relative to this goal is...

I know why I want to achieve this goal. It is because...

How Will I Achieve This Goal?

I will have to overcome the following obstacles and challenges to achieve my goal...

I will need the assistance of the following people to achieve my goal...

I will need the following knowledge and skills to achieve my goal...

I commit to the following specific steps to achieve my goal...

Sample Wealth Creation Goal Sheet

The specific money making or wealth creation goal I will achieve is...

To save a three-month emergency fund of $5,000.

I will achieve this goal by the following date...

24 months from today
My current status/situation relative to this goal is ...

My after tax monthly income is $1,700. I also owe $300 on my credit card.

I know why I want to achieve this goal. It is because ...

I want to stop living in fear of losing my job.

How Will I Achieve This Goal?

I will have to overcome the following obstacles and challenges to achieve my goal...

Modify current spending habits to save $200 every month.

I will need the assistance of the following people to achieve my goal...

My spouse or partner to encourage and support my action.
My boss who will deposit $100 per pay cheque (bi-monthly) directly into the new savings account I will set up.

I will need the following knowledge and skills to achieve my goal...

Investigate available mutual fund accounts.
Develop the discipline to contribute monthly to your funds.
Insure adequate income protection (Term life insurance) in place.

I commit to the following specific steps to achieve my goal...

Cut up department store credit cards.
Take lunch from home at least once a week.

Wealth Creation Action Plan

Goal: *Set up a three-month emergency fund.*

Day One: *Discuss goal with partner or spouse.*

Day Two: *Speak to boss regarding payroll deduction.*

Day Three: *Go to bank, gather information on available funds.*

Day Four: *Visit bank with partner or spouse to open mutual fund.*

Day Five: *Take lunch to work. After dinner conduct credit card cutting ceremony.*

Day Six: *Review past week's accomplishments and celebrate.*

Day Seven: *Day off — rest.*

Week Two: *Get ride to work or use public transportation for at least one day to save on gas and parking.*

Week Three: *Find other cost cutting measures.*

Week Four: *Review past month's efforts, revise next month's plan if necessary. Celebrate successes to date.*

Let's review what we have discussed in this chapter. Our starting point is the assumption that we have given up our old wealth-limiting beliefs and are now becoming a Money Magnet. This section is about getting our behaviors in sync with those of wealthy people. It is about taking our new attitudes and putting them into action as daily behaviors. At first, some of these behaviors may be difficult but that is not necessarily a bad thing. Achieving a goal too easily will not seem like such a great accomplishment. If it hurts a little it is actually a sign that you are stepping out of your familiar comfort zone and growing from within. If you are having a major problem getting started, relax, this is not a race. You should only do this at a pace you find comfortable. Just try not to be too easy on yourself. If it is seeming impossible and you are tempted to give up, then consider rereading the first section on attitudes and making sure that you have actually rid yourself of the wealth-limiting beliefs that have been holding you back.

Remember persistence. If you are constantly running out of steam, if procrastination is beckoning, if your self-discipline is stuck in the detention hall, then a quick review of your Wealth Creation Goal Sheet should turbo- charge your commitment. If it does not then perhaps the goal is no longer as significant or important to you as it once was. Life changes. Not a problem. Move on, set a new goal for yourself.

Here is a summary of some of the important questions you need to answer prior to moving on to Chapter 4, Behaving Frugally: Make Yourself Rich, Not Someone Else.

1. What is Reality Immersion?
2. How can the Reality Immersion concept of "fake it till you make it" work for me?
3. What books, magazines, newspapers, websites, blogs etc., do I plan to read to assist me in becoming rich?
4. What seminars or workshops will I attend to become wealthier?
5. Who do I need to attract to my mastermind team?
6. Why should I bother setting wealth goals? What's in it for me?

7. What S.M.A.R.T. goals do I need to set and achieve to succeed?
8. When will I commit to complete my Wealth Creation Action Plan?

Now that you have focused on your goals and started to mould your actions to be consistent with that pursuit, it is time to look at the specific behaviors that need changing.

Not only does the wealthy person have a realistic set of goals that he or she is pursuing, they also know how to make the money they currently have go further. Chapter 4 outlines how living frugally to make yourself rich does not have to be painful.

Behaving Frugally
Make Yourself Rich,
Not Someone Else

Many people believe that the answer to all their financial problems is simply to have more money. We often hear the expression, "Everything would be better if I could only get a ten per cent raise." The problem with this is that most people live beyond their means. They typically manage to outspend their income by between five and ten per cent. Someone once told us, only partly facetiously, "It does not matter whether you earn $100 per week or $1,000 per week, you are still going to be $38 short at the end of the month. It is a universal law." American consumer debt loads are at the highest levels in history and the total of outstanding credit card debt is the highest it has ever been. Interestingly, a large degree of the population has turned to borrowing to finance their retirement contributions.

When people actually receive promotions and pay increases, they quickly develop new life-styles and are once again living beyond their means. This can become what we call the Money Minimizers' Maze. They used to call this "Owing your soul to the company store." In many cases companies pay their employees just enough money so they do not leave the job to seek employment elsewhere. As this person continues to work, the company rewards them with small promotions and minute pay increases. The problem is compounded by corporate and cultural pressures placed upon the individual to spend more money on fancier clothes, better cars and bigger houses as befits the higher job positions. The maze comes as the person loses his or her independence. They cannot afford to leave the job and accompanying life-style or take time off to realign their life.

All wealthy people know the value of being self disciplined in their personal spending habits. They understand the need to delay instant gratification in their personal spending. These people do not view saving as a painful process. Instead, they see it simply as delayed spending. Successful people realize that until you have your own financial situation in order, the goal should not be to increase income, but to first live better and smarter within your existing income.

Everywhere you turn, someone is trying to entice you into spending more money. In fact, the economy for the most part heavily relies on consumers doing just that. The media is the prime culprit in the indoctrination of the public to believe that those who have money spend lavishly and if you do not show the material trappings of wealth, then you are not really wealthy. Some of the most popular television shows are built entirely around the premise of instant gratification. The shows that we are referring to are the game shows that offer the average member of the audience an opportunity to win from a huge array of conspicuous gifts all packaged up in a neat format. The appeal to the viewer is that an average person just like them can win a boat, car, major appliance, vacation or money in less than an hour with no real effort. This is of tremendous interest to the average person because it feeds on their deep-rooted desire for instant gratification. If the show was reformatted for Money Magnets, the prizes would be: tuition scholarships, business start-up grants, two weeks of free business consulting services, free legal services to incorporate your business or free lunch with your favorite wealth mentor. This show would resonate with an audience of Money Magnets; the only problem is that Money Magnets watch very little television and the little that they do watch is mostly news, documentaries and the occasional sitcom or drama. The result would be that this newly formatted game show would be quickly pulled off the air.

Thomas J. Stanley and William D. Danko have spent most of their adult lives studying the daily habits of self-made millionaires and their research very clearly demonstrates the frugal behavior shared by virtually all wealthy people. They have determined that 75 per cent of all American millionaires have never spent more than $599 for a suit, $199 for a pair of shoes or $1,125 for a watch. So who is buying all these life-style items? It is the moderate - to high - income earning Money Minimizers who are buying these life-style items (usually on credit), trying to look like they are wealthy and in doing so never seem to have any money left over to invest in real income producing assets.

It is about time we learned how to spend less money. Cutting down on expenses is something many of us are unaccustomed to. It seems so foreign and is likely to be very painful. As you will see, it does not have to be that way.

Some of the best role models of frugal behavior are our senior citizens, particularly those who spent their formative years as children during the Great Depression. The sense of cutting back, tightening the belt and saving for a rainy day is as fresh and real in their minds as it was decades ago. This generation very clearly understands the difference between "wants" and "needs." They are in a sense the unsung heroes of frugality.

Many people confuse income and wealth. *Income is what you earn; wealth is how much you keep and accumulate.* Poor and middle class people spend their lives working for money to buy things that make them look like they have money, but these things really do not make them any money.

> We buy things we don't need with money we
> don't have to impress people we don't know.
>
> – Anonymous

Webster's defines frugal as "behavior characterized by or reflecting economy in the use of resources." The opposite of frugal is wasteful. We define the wasteful life-style of a Money Minimizer as being preoccupied with lavish spending and hyper-consumerism. Frugality is a cornerstone of wealth creation.

FINANCIAL FREEDOM SNAPSHOT

To get a quick "picture" of your current financial situation, take a few moments and answer "Yes" or "No" to each of the following statements. Then score yourself using the key on the next page.

1. I often feel stressed out or frustrated with my financial situation.

2. I don't use the services of a trusted, skilled financial advisor.

3. I don't maximize contributions to my IRA orother retirement plan.

4. I pay more than 20% of my income on credit card charges.

5. Unopened bills or notices seem to pile up at home.

6. Several past due or account in arrears notices have arrived in the mail within the past 6 months.

7. If I lost my current source of income things would be very difficult because I don't have a safety net of three month's savings.

8. If I died today my family would experience a financial crisis.

9. My spouse/partner and I don't work on financial issues together.

10. My spouse/partner has no idea about the cost of living.

11. My spouse/partner and I don't have specific financial plans/goals in writing.

12. My spouse/partner and I often disagree about money matters.

13. My checkbook is usually in a negative balance.

14. I can never seem to keep up; this month's bills arrive before I can pay off last month's bills.

15. I usually buy products on installment plans with "nothing down."

16. I feel powerless and without options when it comes to money issues.

17. I occasionally find myself having to borrow money from friends or family.

18. Financial stress seems to affect my health and or cause a lack of sleep.

19. My credit cards are usually "maxed out."

20. I often wish for a 10% pay increase so all my problems would disappear.

21. I regularly buy lottery tickets or gamble.

22. I have only one source of income.

23. Three or more of my checks per year get returned as "Insufficient Funds."

24. I often blame others for my financial problems.

25. I don't know where to start to fix my money problems.

Scoring: Add up all the numbers, then multiply the total x 4.

25 - 39: Your Financial Fitness Snapshot "picture" is quite positive. Your primary objective should be to fine-tune your strategies and further develop your wealth picture.

40 – 75: Your Financial Fitness Snapshot "picture" is slightly better than average. You are doing more things right than wrong, however there certainly are areas that could be improved. Your main focus should be to review your weaker areas and resolve to change them.

76 - 100: Your Financial Fitness Snapshot "picture" is poor. Don't despair, you are not alone. This book was written to assist the 90% of the population that fall into this category.

Have you ever wondered where all your money goes? You work hard, get paid and before you know it all your money has disappeared. Most of us have some sense of what we spend our money on, but only by doing a more detailed budget can we pinpoint the exact places where savings and gains can be made. After determining where the money goes you can categorize your spending into the following: Money Makers (building your money-making asset base), Necessities (food, clothing and shelter) and Wealth Robbers.

ANOTHER WAY TO LOOK AT BUDGETING

Just the very mention of the "B" word is enough to send most adults cowering. One day we decided to stop several average-looking people on the street and, after assuring them we were not trying to sell them anything, we asked them to give us the first thoughts that entered their minds on the subject of budgeting. Here is a sampling:

- Do not talk to me about budgets, what I need is more money.
- Budgets are too restrictive for my life-style.
- Who has the time to budget?
- Budgets are too complicated.
- Budgets are just fancy ways to track past spending.
- My spouse and I are not disciplined enough to stay on a budget.
- Budgeting is a good idea, someday I must get around to doing one.

Apart from having some fun and meeting some interesting people, this exercise simply reinforced the need to work quickly on this book. These average people fit the description of our Money Minimizers so we thought we would try the same thing with friends and associates fitting the Money Magnets description and we got these responses:

- The lack of money is seldom the real issue; the problem is almost always a lack of budgeting.
- It's *your* budget; you can make it as rigid or as flexible as you want.
- It only takes a short while once a week to maintain a budget.
- Budgets do not need to be complicated, in fact some of the most powerful are quite simple.
- A budget is simply a plan to control future spending.
- If you and your spouse are committed to the budget, it can become a habit within three weeks.
- Considering that what you are talking about will improve your day-to-day life, start budgeting now!

Incorporating more frugal behavior into your life does not have to involve a lot of pain. In fact, once you get the hang of it, you can turn it into a profitable game. Take the example of Annica and Tim who approached us, desperate for help, about two years ago. When we first met them they were a very typical couple. They were both educated professionals who lived outside a major city. They had two teenagers, one 15 and the other 13 years old, two cars, both in need of repairs, and lived in a modest house with an $89,000 mortgage. They made small annual contributions to their IRA and did not live a lavish life-style. As Tim said: "Our annual raises are ahead of the inflation rate but we still seem to struggle from pay check to pay check. The only beneficiary of our hard work, overtime and raises is the government. It is not like we take expensive annual family vacations travelling through Europe, we usually just spend holidays at home working around the house." Annica added: "The chances of us starting up a proper investment account are between slim and none as every penny is already spoken for. It is not like we are not working hard enough, we barely have time as it is to talk to each other or our kids with our demanding schedules."

If we have heard this story once we have heard it hundreds of times. As with almost any problem the first part of the cure is to realize that you have a problem and then seek out help to solve it. Annica practically solved her own problem and that of literally millions of others, when she said: "We just cannot figure out where it all goes." The first step, then, was to do a snapshot of how they spend their money using a form like the one we developed and have conveniently supplied – the Monthly Money Monitor.

Examining this financial awareness statement, Annica and Tim were surprised to see just how much money they spent on items that were not very highly valued. We started with their telephones. They helped keep the phone company in business with two phone lines and two cell phones. The second line was primarily for the use of their kids who, like their parents, were not home very much. Now seemed like a good time to get rid of one line. As both their kids were teenagers with small incomes from part-time jobs, if they really needed their own phone line that much they could pay for it themselves and start to learn the value of money. This seemed to us a perfect segue into a much bigger area. Part of Annica and Tim's problem was that neither of them had learned appropriate wealth building strategies while they were growing up and were, inadvertently, passing on these bad habits to their children. We convinced them to discuss the whole situation openly and honestly with their children and to make them part of the decision-making process.

The initial discussion went well but we needed a device to get the kids more committed. We came up with the idea of making the children mini-consultants for the family "company." Using a simple pay-for-performance incentive scheme we got the kids involved in discovering ways to save money around the home. For every dollar saved or generated they would get 20 cents to spend on whatever they wanted. The first idea was to clean out the closets of old toys, games and clothes for a lawn sale which netted the kids $65. The next idea the kids came up with was to save on energy by ensuring that nobody left the lights, televisions, air-conditioners or computers turned on unnecessarily.

Looking again at their phones, there was also a monthly long distance plan fee that they were not really benefiting from. Dropping the plan meant they spent an average of an extra dollar per month on calls but the net savings was $4 per month. It may not seem like much, but every little bit counts and can add up by the end of the year. Two cell phones was also an unnecessary luxury. Annica's part-time schedule was more erratic and she drove the car that was more likely to break down, so she kept the one phone during the week and gave it to Tim when he ran errands on the weekend. They also decided to drop the add-ons like voice messaging, call waiting and call display on the remaining phone. By the end of the month the savings were $50 on cell phones, $20 for the residential line and $4 for the long distance plan. A total of $74 just for telephones!

They had two desktop computers and one laptop. The kids shared one computer for homework assignments; Annica and Tim used one primarily for e-mail. The kids had a high speed Internet connection while the parents had a dial-up account. The laptop collected dust. They decided to sell the laptop for $300 and buy a Networking card and cable to connect the two remaining computers for a onetime net profit of $150. Now they could send files to the kid's computer for sending e-mail and drop the dial up connection for a savings of $21 every month.

After keeping a log of everyone's favorite television programs for two weeks they found that with one exception, everything they watched was on the basic level of their cable subscription. This coincided with a realization that they were not watching as much television as they once did, partly because they were involved in so many other activities and much of what they were doing was simply "killing time" in front of the box. They eliminated the higher two tiers and the premium movie channels for a savings of $30 per month. This now meant that they had to go out and rent movies on the occasion that they actually wanted to watch one. The good part of this was that they got to pick the movies they really wanted to see rather than waste time watching what was available through their subscription. This cost was accounted for in their entertainment budget. Instead of going to a theatre and paying premium prices plus parking and junk food, they now made it a family evening at home with a rental at a fraction of the cost. For the few "must see" current movies they resolved to go to the reduced cost matinees or "Cheap Tuesdays."

Part and parcel of being so busy was that newspapers and magazines hit the recycling box without being opened. The two daily newspapers were cut back to one for a savings of $30; an industry magazine which could be read for free at the office saved another $5 per month; two life-style magazines were reduced to one for another monthly savings of $5 and instead of a weekly television schedule magazine at $5 month, the free insert in the Saturday paper could do the job just as well. The total monthly savings on newspapers and magazines was $45.

Tim had a $60 per month membership at a local gym which, because of his other commitments, he attended only sporadically. He found an aerobics machine for sale in the local "Buy & Sell" for $20 and he set up an exercise area in the basement. He does not use that very much either but he is ahead by $60 every month.

Over the years the family had collected quite a pile of "treasures" that they never used but could not seem to part with. Their garage was so full that they had to rent storage space on a monthly basis for $25. The decision was made to empty out both the garage and shed and have a yard sale. The sale netted $612 and resulted in cancelling the monthly rental (and reducing the fire-hazard in the garage). The net savings was $25.

Changing food and alcohol habits were more challenging. Instead of two $90 monthly meals at their favorite restaurant, they cut back to one meal out. They replaced that second night out with a trip to the gourmet shop and bought some prepared meals. Together with a better bottle of wine than they would get at the restaurant, they were ahead by $50. As the gourmet meal and the wine actually tasted a little better, there was a serious discussion about saving the restaurant for special occasions like birthdays and anniversaries and pocketing the savings. The fact that they were enjoying themselves just as much while simultaneously putting their financial house in order, made the food and wine taste just that much better.

The couple also started participating in a Saturday night Financial Food for Thought program with their neighbors, that we will describe later in the Stretching a Dollar section. This also saved them a considerable sum. For our purposes here we are only going to deal with the above black and white savings which totalled $305 per month or $3,660 every year (see Tim and Annica's Family for a summary). If Tim and Annica took the $305 per month they saved (paid on the first day of each month) and invested it at eight per cent, it would amount to a $55,291.88 nest-egg at the end of only ten years. Leave it growing for 20 years and the amount becomes a very respectable $174,661.31.

Annica and Tim were thrilled. The cuts did not hurt very much at all and in fact after two months of getting used to it, they wondered how they ever managed to justify their previously "lavish" life-style. Not only was it painless, but it was actually a lot of fun knowing that they were now in a much healthier financial position.

We now had to take Tim and Annica through a process that would require more effort, discipline and commitment. Having made it this far we knew they were ready to accelerate their wealth-building adventure. The next step meant they needed to engage in another round of creative frugal thinking. The degree to which they decided to cut back on costly items such as clothes, manicures and the second car meant it would have a profound impact on building future wealth. From now on, everything they decided to spend their hard-earned dollars on would be subjected to some very tough scrutiny. This resulted in them now being in control of their financial futures rather than helplessly floundering on Tim's unused treadmill.

Tim and Annica's Family

Monthly Money Monitor – Summary Statement

Reductions in Monthly Expenses	Dollars Saved per Month
Telephone	$74
Internet connection	$21
Cable television rates	$30
Subscriptions (Newspapers and Magazines)	$45
Gym membership	$60
Storage space rental	$25
Dining out	$50
Total reduction in monthly expenses	**$ 305**

Now it's your turn. A lot of people share Tim and Annica's position: You earn $1,000 over a certain amount of time and your cost of living during that period is, if you're lucky, $998 or $1,038 if you're not. There's little or no breathing room. So, the first thing to do is examine carefully where it all goes. We want to help you track your fixed monthly expenses. On the Monthly Money Monitor, fill in the amount you pay for your rent/mortgage, electricity, phone and all the other expenses you are obligated to pay each month on the forms which follow. This chart may seem complex but when you read it you'll find it's really easy to complete. If you don't have to pay for electricity, for example, leave it blank and move on. We've included just about every conceivable expense so that you don't miss any. For annual costs such as house repairs, take the total cost and divide it by twelve. If you don't know the exact number, make a good guess.

Monthly Money Monitor

Month: _____ of 20_____

Monthly Expense Planner Monthly (Accommodation)	Person #1	Person #2	Person #3	Total
Mortgage, Rent or Room and Board				
Property Taxes				
Repairs and Maintenance				
Improvements				
Home Insurance or Tenants Insurance				
Electricity				
Natural Gas				
Heating Oil				
Water				
Telephone				
Internet Connection				
Cable				
Sanitation				
Appliances Repair or Upgrade				
Other				
Subtotal Accommodations Expenses				

Monthly Money Monitor

Month: _____ of 20_____

Monthly Expense Planner Monthly (Automobile)	Person # 1	Person # 2	Person # 3	Total
Loan or Lease Payments				
Repairs and Maintenance				
Fuel and Oil				
Registration and Licensing				
Insurance				
Parking				
Other				
Subtotal Automobiles Expenses				

Monthly Money Monitor

Month: _____ of 20_____

Monthly Expense Planner Monthly (Financial)	Person # 1	Person # 2	Person # 3	Total
Savings				
Life, Health, Medical and Disability Insurance				
Investment Payments				
IRA Contributions				
Credit Card # 1				
Credit Card # 2				
Credit Card # 3				
Credit Card # 4				
Credit Card # 5				
Loan Payment				
Alimony or Child Support Payment				
Other				
Subtotal Financial Expenses				

Monthly Money Monitor

Month: _____ of 20_____

Monthly Expense Planner Monthly (Family and Personal Expenses)	Person # 1	Person # 2	Person # 3	Total
Groceries				
Eating Out				
Medical Prescriptions, Vitamins and Natural Remedies				
Professional Fees: Doctor, Dentist, Chiropractor and Natural Health Practitioner				
Clothing				
Laundry and Dry Cleaning				
School/University Supplies				
Entertainment				
Baby-sitters				
Day Care/After School Programme				
Child Recreation Fees				
Allowances				
Tuition Fees/Course Costs				
Memberships				
Travel				
Vacation				
Pet Food and Care				
Beauty, Barber Shop, Toiletry and Cosmetics				
Gifts				
Donations				
Tithing				
Other				
Subtotal Family and Personal Expenses				
Total Monthly Expenses				

Now that you've filled out this chart, get creative. Analyze all of the expenses and ask yourself whether you could reduce or live without some of them. Do you really need the cellphone? Perhaps you do, but do you need unlimited talk time? Maybe a minimum plan would suffice just so you have service in emergencies or when you're running late. You may save $20 to $30 per month. Do you need all of those cable channels? Maybe the basic plan would give you what you *really* need and encourage more reading or physical activity. Are you paying off credit card debts at 18 or 28 per cent? Get a basic credit card that allows you to transfer debts and start paying the lower amount. Or, pay the same amount each month and get rid of the debt quicker.

Now, here's the most important part of the exercise: If you find a way to save $20 or more every month, put that amount into a savings plan so that it starts to work for you.

Having completed this exercise it's time for the next step – your day to day spending habits. Here is a sample diary of how someone typically spends their cash from day to day. As you can see, it adds up quickly and represents a substantial expense.

Daily Money Monitor – Sample

Monday	Expense	Tuesday	Expense
Coffee & donut	3.99	Coffee & donut	3.99
Newspaper	1.00	Newspaper	1.00
Juice & muffin	4.50	Snack	3.50
Lunch	6.50	Lunch	6.00
Magazine	5.00	Snack	3.00
Candy bar	1.50	Gas	25.00
Gas	30.00	Groceries	40.00
Milk, bread, fruit	9.50	Dance club admission	15.00
Drinks after work	22.50	Drinks	25.00
		Taxi home	22.00
Totals	**84.49**	**Totals**	**144.49**

Make some copies of Daily Money Monitor and fill it in every night before you go to bed – it's much easier to remember if you do it every day – over the course of a week or more. These exercises work whether you earn $1,000 a year or $100,000 a year. **It's not about how much you make, it's what you do with it that counts.**

Daily Money Monitor

Monday	Expense

Tuesday	Expense

Wednesday	Expense

Thursday	Expense

Friday   Expense

Saturday   Expense

Sunday   Expense

Now let's look at where you spend your money. Could you drink your coffee at home and save those few dollars every day? If your purchase includes a pastry you may end up doing your heart a great service in the process. How much would you save by bringing a sandwich for lunch? Are you spending $20 per day on gasoline? How about car pooling with a friend or neighbor or taking public transport once a week? If the magazine you buy is essential reading you could probably save at least 50% of the cost by taking out a subscription. Meeting friends at a bar is great for unwinding after work. Why not try meeting in a coffee bar where the drinks are significantly cheaper or going to a park with a juice? There are many other examples, the point is to first identify where the money goes. You will probably be surprised at how much you spend and how easy it is to save money on a regular basis. Lots of people get into the habit of throwing their loose change into a jar at the end of every day. After a month they are amazed at the amount. Remember, the key here is to put that extra money into a savings account and get it working for you.

Now that you've started to think more economically you'll really appreciate the next section of the book which lists loads of cost cutting measures you may not have considered yet. Before we get to that, we want you to get an overall "snapshot" of your present financial position. To achieve this, fill in the Net Worth Planner – Current Assets chart.

After you've completed that exercise fill in the next chart, the Net Worth Planner – Liabilities. Then take the total of your Current Assets chart and subtract the total of your Liabilities chart. This is a tool designed to help you accomplish two things:

1. Determine your current level of wealth.
2. Serve as a tool to plan specific wealth goals.

By completing the column labelled "today" on each page you will be able to calculate three things:

1. The total current value of what you own – your assets.
2. The total current amount of what you owe – your liabilities or debts.
3. The net difference between the two is your wealth or net worth. The higher the number, the wealthier you are.

This tool does not tell the story of how you arrived at this financial situation, or where it's headed. It merely describes your
current position. Just as with the daily and monthly "Money Monitors" it is only when we see our financial reality in black and white in front of us that we begin to see the bigger picture of where we are headed. If you're not happy with that direction, then there's a better chance of changing it.

Secondly, by filling in the columns "six months," "one year" etc., you can plot specific goals for the future in each category. The idea is that over time your assets will increase while your liabilities decrease, thus you will become wealthier with a high level of net worth.

The Short-term Debt Buster which follows the Net Worth Planner is a tool that quickly identifies which of your debts are costing the most in terms of higher interest rates. The quickest way to reduce debt is to pay off the debts with the highest rate of interest. Then you pay off the debts with lower interest rates. The goal, of course, is to eventually become debt-free. In the process of paying off your debts you want to minimize the interest payments and maximize the principal payments.

One way that this can be accelerated is to consolidate all of your higher interest debts into one low interest payment. Combining payments makes it a lot easier to budget. (One monthly payment versus many, plus more of the payment will go towards reducing the amount owing or principal. The best consolidation loans are those that allow for extra payments or early payout without any penalties. Several credit card companies offer a low interest (6–8%) card on which they will allow you to transfer balances from other higher interest cards. The Short-term Debt Buster chart (see page 92) shows an example of this consolidation. Above it is a blank worksheet for your own use.

Net Worth Planner – Current Assets

	Today	6 Months	1 Year	2 Years	5 Years	10 Years	20 Years
Cash in Checking/Savings Accounts							
Account # Bank/Branch	$	$	$	$	$	$	$
Account # Bank/Branch	$	$	$	$	$	$	$
Account # Bank/Branch	$	$	$	$	$	$	$
Non-Registered Investments – CDs Held							
Certificate # Fin. Institution	$	$	$	$	$	$	$
Certificate # Fin. Institution	$	$	$	$	$	$	$
Certificate # Fin. Institution	$	$	$	$	$	$	$
Government Savings Bonds Held							
Certificate # Fin. Institution	$	$	$	$	$	$	$
Certificate # Fin. Institution	$	$	$	$	$	$	$
Certificate # Fin. Institution	$	$	$	$	$	$	$
Treasury Bills Held							
Certificate #	$	$	$	$	$	$	$
Certificate #	$	$	$	$	$	$	$
Stocks, Common or Preferred; Mutual Funds							
Portfolio Value	$	$	$	$	$	$	$
Registered Investments – CDs Held							
Certificate # Fin. Institution	$	$	$	$	$	$	$
Certificate # Fin. Institution	$	$	$	$	$	$	$
Certificate # Fin. Institution	$	$	$	$	$	$	$
Registered Government Savings Bonds Held							
Certificate # Fin. Institution	$	$	$	$	$	$	$
Certificate # Fin. Institution	$	$	$	$	$	$	$
Certificate # Fin. Institution	$	$	$	$	$	$	$
Registered Treasury Bills Held							
Certificate #	$	$	$	$	$	$	$
Certificate #	$	$	$	$	$	$	$
Registered Stocks or Mutual Funds							
Portfolio Value	$	$	$	$	$	$	$
Subtotal Current Assets	$	$	$	$	$	$	$

Net Worth Planner – Other Assets

		Today	6 Months	1 Year	2 Years	5 Years	10 Years	20 Years
Insurance Policies Held								
Policy Insurer	Cash Value	$	$	$	$	$	$	$
Policy Insurer	Cash Value	$	$	$	$	$	$	$
Policy Insurer	Cash Value	$	$	$	$	$	$	$
Mortgage Held								
Debtor	Net Value	$	$	$	$	$	$	$
Loans Held								
Debtor	Net Value	$	$	$	$	$	$	$
Debtor	Net Value	$	$	$	$	$	$	$
Personal Real Estate								
Principal Residence	Fair Market Value	$	$	$	$	$	$	$
Cottage	Fair Market Value	$	$	$	$	$	$	$
Other	Fair Market Value	$	$	$	$	$	$	$
Investment/Business Real Estate								
Property # 1	Fair Market Value	$	$	$	$	$	$	$
Property # 2	Fair Market Value	$	$	$	$	$	$	$
Vehicles								
Automobile # 1	Fair Market Value	$	$	$	$	$	$	$
Automobile # 2	Fair Market Value	$	$	$	$	$	$	$
Automobile # 3	Fair Market Value	$	$	$	$	$	$	$
Boat	Fair Market Value	$	$	$	$	$	$	$
Other	Fair Market Value	$	$	$	$	$	$	$
Other Assets								
Jewellery/Furs		$	$	$	$	$	$	$
Art		$	$	$	$	$	$	$
Furniture/Household Effects		$	$	$	$	$	$	$
Business Inventory		$	$	$	$	$	$	$
Accounts Receivable		$	$	$	$	$	$	$
Other	$	$	$	$	$	$	$	$
Subtotal Other Assets		$	$	$	$	$	$	$
Total All Assets		$	$	$	$	$	$	$

Net Worth Planner – Liabilities

	Today	6 Months	1 Year	2 Years	5 Years	10 Years	20 Years
Credit Card Balances							
Credit Card # 1 Interest Rate %	$	$	$	$	$	$	$
Credit Card # 2 Interest Rate %	$	$	$	$	$	$	$
Credit Card # 3 Interest Rate %	$	$	$	$	$	$	$
Credit Card # 4 Interest Rate %	$	$	$	$	$	$	$
Credit Card # 5 Interest Rate %	$	$	$	$	$	$	$
Current Bills Payable							
Bill # 1	$	$	$	$	$	$	$
Bill # 2	$	$	$	$	$	$	$
Bill # 3	$	$	$	$	$	$	$
Loans Balances							
Car # 1	$	$	$	$	$	$	$
Car # 2	$	$	$	$	$	$	$
Other	$	$	$	$	$	$	$
Other	$	$	$	$	$	$	$
Personal Real Estate Mortgage Balances							
Principal Residence Pay Out Balance	$	$	$	$	$	$	$
Cottage Pay Out Balance	$	$	$	$	$	$	$
Other Pay Out Balance	$	$	$	$	$	$	$
Investment/Business Real Estate Mortgage							
Property # 1 Pay Out Balance	$	$	$	$	$	$	$
Property # 2 Pay Out Balance	$	$	$	$	$	$	$
Taxes Payable							
Income Tax	$	$	$	$	$	$	$
Property Taxes	$	$	$	$	$	$	$
Business Liabilities							
Accounts Payable	$	$	$	$	$	$	$
Business Loan	$	$	$	$	$	$	$
Other	$	$	$	$	$	$	$
Subtotal Liabilities	$	$	$	$	$	$	$
Total Net Worth (Total Assets Minus Liabilities)	$	$	$	$	$	$	$

Short-term Debt Buster

Type of Debt		Interest Rate %	Pay Out Balance	Credit Limit	Monthly Payment
Credit Card # 1	His Visa	18.5	$2,900	$3,000	$145.00
Credit Card # 2	His Master Card	18.5	$1,500	$1,500	$75.00
Credit Card # 3	Her Visa	18.5	$4,800	$5,000	$240.00
Credit Card # 4	Her Master Card	18.5	$1,600	$2,000	$80.00
Credit Card # 5	Furniture Store	29.5	$1,700	$2,500	$85.00
Credit Card # 6	Departmental Store	24.5	$990	$1,000	$50.00
Credit Card # 7	Gas Card	24.5	$450	$500	$15.00
Personal Loan	Car	12.0	$15,330	$20,000 (borrowed)	$664.20
Other	Bank line of credit	12.0	$2,560	$20,000	$128.00
Totals			$31,830		$1,482.20

After a Consolidation of Debts (Closing the $20,000 line of credit and opening a $16,500 3-year Loan at 12% interest.)

Type of Debt		Interest Rate %	Pay Out Balance	Credit Limit	Monthly Payment
Personal Loan # 1	Car	12.0	$15,330	$20,000 (borrowed)	$664.20
Personal Loan # 2	Consolidation	12.0	$16,500	$16,500 (borrowed)	$547.97
Totals			$31,830		$1,212.17
Amount saved/available for investing					$270.03

Note: This sample is for illustration purposes only. The rate of interest will vary. Visa and MasterCard are registered trademarks.

Short-term Debt Buster Worksheet

Type of Debt	Interest Rate Charged	Pay Out Balance	Monthly Payment
Credit Card # 1			
Credit Card # 2			
Credit Card # 3			
Credit Card # 4			
Credit Card # 5			
Personal Loan # 1			
Personal Loan # 2			
Personal Loan # 3			
Other			
Other			
Totals			

LEARNING TO STRETCH A DOLLAR

The following are just a few money saving suggestions. The point is to start you thinking about and re-examining the way you spend money. Using even one suggestion will save you money. Hopefully this will stimulate you to re-examine everything you spend and ultimately behave more frugally. As you go through these ask yourself what your life would be like without the cell phone, for example. If you are a real estate agent or a free-lance cameraman, then you probably depend on it for your business. For others, it may be a nonessential luxury. You probably lived without one for many years. There are still payphones on many corners. Just consider it. If it is essential, spend the money; if it is a toy, put the money to better use in a savings plan. There are hundreds more ideas. E-mail us the ones that work for you at info@abcsofmakingmoney.com.

Barter Instead of Bucks

Try bartering for services when you cannot afford the cash outlay. Investigate whether you have a skill that would be considered valuable to the person from whom you are trying to make a purchase. Check your local tax laws to prevent future problems.

Frugality is in Fashion

When buying clothes, shop mid to end of season. Fashions are still current but cheaper. Independent clothiers can negotiate up to five per cent discount on cash sales rather than credit cards. For a man, with a good quality pair of black jeans and shoes you can have a good casual look. Add a belt and a shirt and you are ready for the club scene; change the belt and add dress shoes, with a dress shirt and a sport coat and your ready for business. It does not have to be expensive. With a few basic items and some inexpensive accessories you now have a versatile wardrobe.

Home Economics

- Get a co-renter or offer "room and board" to offset the cost of part of your home.
- Ask for a reassessment. Alan remembers: "A little over a year ago I received a notice of reassessment for my house. The good news was that in the city's professional opinion my house was worth double the amount it had been previously assessed, based on current market values. The bad news was that I would soon be paying taxes on the higher value, but not getting any additional municipal services. Apart from the increased expense in the short term, it would also make the house less desirable to a future purchaser, from a taxation perspective. So I called the city and told them I disagreed with their assessment. The city supplied me with comparable assessment values for all of my neighbors with similar sized properties. A local real estate agent gave me a copy of all the recent local home sales. With these two bits of information I was able to successfully argue that my property tax assessment should be lower. I was reassessed at $100,000 less, which resulted in a real tax savings of $400 per year. This exercise cost me about one half hour on the phone and another 30 minutes to write a letter. I learned later that it was not so much the brilliance of my argument but

the fact that very few people actually went to the trouble of complaining. Almost everyone who did received a savings.

- Do-It-Yourself type large home building centres give free how-to seminars for the home fixer. Help a neighbor. "I will help fix your patio if you help me paint my deck." Buy a case of beer for a friend to help fix your plumbing leak. Tip: Fix the leak before you drink the beer!

The Power of Frugality

Set up timers and turn off lights when leaving rooms. Buy and use a setback thermostat. Add some insulation; do some caulking and window repairs to save cold or hot air from escaping your home. Replace a traditional fireplace with an airtight insert. If you are going to burn a tree, why not use it efficiently? Also, add an inexpensive blower to maximize the warm air into your home. Turn off air-conditioners when not in the rooms. In warm climates try a ceiling fan.

Money Down the Drain

Get rain barrel collectors for your gardens. Some communities give them away for free. No shower should be longer than five minutes. Save money on bottled water; buy a NSF-approved activated carbon-water filtration system (approximately $10) and maintain your health. Refill empty bottles for looking and feeling cool. Stop all leaky taps, do not be a financial drip.

Financial Food for Thought

Grow your own vegetables in your back yard or a community cooperative garden. It is healthy, fun and saves money. Home preserving is good. Buying in bulk, generic or "no name" can represent incredible value for a low price point. Eating out is fun but expensive. Consider organizing a group of friends to do a rotation event. Go to a different friend's place every week or month with each person bringing a part of the meal. You get a social experience, a break from the monotony of home-cooked meals and save on the restaurant bills. When going to the restaurant cut back on the alcohol component and save up to half the bill. If you enjoy wine or beer consider home brewing. It is fun, the quality is quite high and approximately a third of the price. This allows you to better afford the odd premium-priced bottle for that special occasion.

A Prescription for Your Financial Woes

* Ask your doctor for generic rather than full price medications.
* Quit smoking! As we calculated in the Introduction, someone who kicks this habit wins in three obvious ways. First, depending on the length of their addiction, their health should improve and they may escape a horrific and painful death. Secondly, they will save roughly $6.00 every day. Over 30 years that amounts to $65,700. If the $42.00 saved every week was invested @ 10%, the ex-addict would not only be alive in 30 years, he or she would have an extra $440,491 to spend. Third, monthly premiums are much higher for smokers who buy car, home, life, health and dental insurance.That is a lot of money for ending one bad habit. Imagine if you combined that kind of savings with some of the other advice in this book, then one million dollars doesn't seem so elusive.
* Take advantage of publicly sponsored vaccinations.
* Examine your hospital and doctor bills carefully for hidden charges.
* Investigate health and dental services available for free or low cost at your local medical or dental school.
* Take your own essentials (tissues, toothpaste, reading material etc.) to the hospital.

Run Over on the Information Highway

Get a decent long distance plan for your phone. Re-examine your use of your cell phone.

If you already have a home computer and an inexpensive Internet connection, you can save money on long distance calls by sending e-mails to friends and family, save on newspaper subscriptions, learn about health issues and world events and have fairly inexpensive fun. Sending photographs through the

Net to relatives and friends saves a lot in reprints and snail mail.

For watching "Rich media" events and programs, high speed (broadband) Internet is almost a must. Having said that, unless you're downloading full length movies you don't need the highest - most expensive - speed. Go for something midrange and save. For friends, family and business contacts you can't beat Skype. Along with a $40 webcam you get free video calls.

Cable or satellite rates

Take the basics. Alan says: My wife and I are probably typical of most households these days. We're so busy with work, travel, reading and socializing that we couldn't possibly watch more than an hour ot two of TV in a day. So, why pay for 500 channels when you rarely watch more than a dozen? We only pay for the basic satellite channels and, when we have an evening in, we rent a DVD for $4. Do yourself a favor and keep a log of the channels you and your family watch for a week or two. Do you really need all the channels you're paying for or would a "Basic" package suffice? If your kids complain, supplement your basic package with a single Theme pack and enjoy the savings.

Life in the Fast Lane

The high cost of gas is forcing people to rethink their use of the car. This is a good thing for the budget and the air.

- •Carpooling saves gas, parking passes and the environment.
- •If the math makes sense, ditch the SUV and get a smaller car or hybrid.
- •Use a bike rather than the car.
- •Don't buy frivolous options for your car; it costs more to buy, finance and repair.
- •Slow down, save gas and stay alive.

We are very nationalistic and make an effort to support local businesses. Unfortunately, that conviction does not extend to purchasing an inferior product where a superior one exists.

Other than a house, cars often represent one of the largest purchases for the average consumer. If you are like the average person, you will trade in your car every three to five years. Most people reason that since they are "turning over" cars so frequently the smartest purchase would be a low -to moderate-cost vehicle. The problem is that in most cases this simply does not make good, economic sense.

We both drive BMWs. Not for any status or prestige but because they are very well designed and well built. Alan says: "When I bought my brand new car, many years ago, I paid approximately 20 per cent more than the "equivalent" Japanese or American model. Over the years I have more than recouped this cost. Not to mention the fact that the resale price is protected due to the much lower rate of depreciation. Domestic carmakers change the design of their cars so frequently that an owner quickly looks out of style or out of fashion. This creates a pressure to purchase new cars more often, which is great for the economy, but bad for the consumer. Our cars have a classic look; one that is rarely changed and never looks outdated. In our opinion, most North American cars are not well designed or well engineered, leading to costly and annoying breakdowns almost the minute they are out of warranty. If you cannot afford the price of a new car try to purchase a quality used car, like a BMW, but have an independent mechanic appraise it before you buy."

Any mechanical device will show signs of wear after a number of years but there is no reason that a well-designed, well-built vehicle cannot, if it is looked after, last for ten or more years. When you factor the increased life span, low cost of maintenance, high rate of reliability and high resale value, it makes one realize the value in investing a little bit more money to get quality. While our personal tastes are for BMWs, high marks also go to Volvo, Saab, Mercedes-Benz and many Japanese cars.

Laundering Money and Other Tips on "Cleaning Up"

Laundry and dry cleaning. Buying a washer for your apartment can save money in as little as one year – to say nothing of the convenience. You can get a used machine for very little. If you have a washing machine, you can wash your own shirts and save the money on dry cleaning. If your suit is not dirty but needs the wrinkles removed, hang it up on the rod of your shower and let the steam help you save on the dry cleaning until it actually needs to be cleaned.

Using Kid Gloves

If you are going out with friends and each couple has one or two kids, take one set of kids to the others' house and split the cost of a baby-sitter. This can actually be easier for the baby-sitter if the kids are comfortable with each other because they are hanging out with friends rather than just with the baby-sitter.

Entertaining Ideas

Do you need to see the latest movie the week it comes out with all of the attendant costs of parking, baby-sitters and restaurants? You could wait for a few months, rent the movie, have your friends over so that you include the social element and save huge amounts of money. Let your friends provide the meal, movie and refreshments the next week. If you need to see the latest blockbuster try to make it on a Tuesday night when many theatres offer a discount rate or, perhaps, you can see a matinee and save money. The biggest money saving is probably in avoiding the obscenely overpriced junk food on the way into the movie. It will not do your health any good and is ridiculously priced.

Membership has Its Privileges

Staff at certain clubs or universities can extend free membership to family members. Consider volunteering at a club to gain some free privileges.

Financial Destination Unknown

- Travel off season and try last minute travel; remove the middleman by using the Internet or travel discounters.
- Demand the lowest rate when booking a hotel room. If they have the space available, they will usually bargain against the threat of going to another hotel.
- Take a bus or subway to the airport rather than a taxi.

Avoid Wealth Robbers

This is another set of suggestions, any one of which will save you lots of money. Use this list to stimulate your own ideas and send us your favorites by e-mail to **info@abcguys.com**.

Taking Credit for Your Wealth

Credit cards. Avoid the gold card fees for services you do not benefit from or use. Read the cardholder agreement carefully. You will often find that for the replacement of a lost or stolen item, for example, they cover only the portion that your homeowner or apartment insurance did not cover – which is most, if not all, of it anyway. Extended warranties are also a waste (see the following section).

If you can justify premium cards for business use, then your company should be paying the fees.

Do not use high interest cards. If you have to carry a balance make sure it's on the lowest interest card you can get and not on a department store or gas card.

Minimize the number of cards you have to avoid extra paperwork and time wastage. You are more likely to fall behind on payments if you have multiple cards as you may run out of time to organize the payments. Every time you are late on a payment it costs you money needlessly.

Never take a cash advance unless you have not eaten in a week. That is the most expensive money you can use.

Timing of cash flow. If your card's statement date is the 21st, for example, and you purchase supplies for your business on the 22nd, you will have approximately 40 days of interest free money until you have to pay. If you are in a receivable situation, this timing plan can be a big advantage. The most important thing is that you make sure you pay the debt on the due date to avoid charges. If you can't afford to pay it off, don't buy it.

Call your credit card company and tell them you want a one half to one point reduction on your interest rate or you will take your business elsewhere. The worst they can say is "No."

Avoid Payday Loan companies like the plague. These companies prey upon the people that can least afford their services. They will loan you money against your next pay check but will charge up to 60 per cent for their services in fees, interest and hidden charges. We recently saw a similar situation in which companies would loan people the value of their car. In this case you sign over the ownership of the car to the company until you have paid them back the loan and interest. The problem is that the interest rates are so high that in many cases you end up paying more than double the price of the car. If you fail to make your payment, the lender will repossess your car.

Never borrow money you cannot afford to repay. Read any loan agreement thoroughly and if you do not understand it, have a trusted knowledgeable friend look it over for you. Be aware of hidden charges and costs. If you are not sure, do not sign it. It could cost you a fortune you cannot afford.

Over-Extended Warranties

Electronics. These are priced with such thin margins that the salesperson can only make a small commission on a sale. They can make three times that amount if you buy the extended warranty insurance. Unfortunately, the vast majority of buyers never get any value from this purchase. Electronic equipment tends to malfunction early or very late in its life. The initial period after purchase is usually covered by the manufacturer's warranty. By the time the electronic unit has begun to malfunction, it is probably worth very little and there are newer and better units available. Often the cost of replacement is cheaper than the repair. Read reports for consumers before buying. Often the extra few dollars you pay for a "name" brand like Sony repays itself in years of extra service.

Car warranties. No car manufacturer is going to offer to cover an item on a car that has a high probability of failure. Wear and tear items are not covered in the first place. The extended warranties only cover the things like the power train that will greatly outlast the coverage. Items such as mufflers, suspensions, struts, shock absorbers, radiators and clutches tend to last through the initial warranty period only to fail when that period is up. Guess what's not covered in most extended warranties? Anything likely to wear out. Read the warranty carefully!

The "Lifetime" warranty. Alan writes: "After suffering the cost of a name brand muffler replacement, the next time I needed one I went to an aftermarket supplier. They were less expensive and, most importantly, gave me a 'lifetime' warranty. A few years later, when I heard a noise in the muffler section I drove back to the shop, produced my carefully preserved warranty and asked them to fix my muffler. 'Certainly sir, but the problem is not in the muffler, it is in the pipe leading to the muffler and *it* is not covered by the warranty. Only the muffler itself is.'

The scam is, evidently, to make a muffler practically indestructible and to make the piping in and out of it from something like aluminum foil. Benefiting from my experience, when Denis needed a replacement muffler for his car he checked until he found one that had an integrated tailpipe assembly, all of which was covered under a lifetime warranty."

To serve and Protect. Fabric guarding can cost hundreds of dollars from the manufacturer of cars and furniture. Save yourself this cost by going to a hardware store, buying a can for $6 and spraying the item yourself. Leather protection: Same as above, a $20 kit will cover four leather couches and save you about $250 per couch.

Term financing. Make the payments over the shortest period you can afford. If you can afford to pay in 24 rather than 36 months you will end up paying less over the term. Based on a $5,000 loan and an interest rate of 10%, 24 months of payments will cost $230.72 per month or $5,537.28. Paying the same amount over 36 months will lower the monthly payment to $161.33 but after 36 months you will have paid $5,807.88 or $270.60 more for the convenience of a lower monthly premium. In some cases that makes the most sense but it is lost money. When the amount is greater, such as the payment on a $20,000 or $30,000 car, the costs are significant. Again, if you can only afford the lower monthly premium, your life may be less stressful but you will pay for that lower payment. Now take the example of a department store credit card at 29.5 per cent. Financing a $5,000 purchase over 24 months will cost 278.27 a month or $6,678.48 ($1,678.48 in interest). The same purchase over 36 months cost $210.89 per month or $7,592.04 ($2,592.04 in interest). So, the 24-month payment will save you $913.56 in interest payments

If you can get a year or two year old car, perhaps a demo, which often come loaded with extra features, low mileage, all the bugs worked out and with a transferable warranty, you will save thousands of dollars over a new one.

Insurance Smarts

Why do most people need life insurance? To protect against the loss of a bread winners' earnings in the event of death. You have to ask the question: "Are there any people dependent on my income?" For example, the single person with no immediate plans for marriage and who has no children or other dependents has no need for life insurance even if he or she owns real estate. This will be covered later in the book. Beyond the obvious grief of friends and loved ones, no one will suffer financially if this person dies. If someone on the other hand has or soon will have dependents, then it is a very wise financial move to acquire sufficient life insurance.

What types of life insurance do you want to avoid?

Credit life insurance

This is tied to your credit card, car loans and mortgages. These are offered at the time of applying for the credit device. The application will normally contain a tick-the-box section that will automatically cover the outstanding balance of the debt should the holder die. The problem is that it is an incredibly expensive price to pay for the amount of coverage you actually receive. Consider Term life insurance and get much higher coverage for a lower fee than what the credit provider will be offering. The second problem is the declining balance situation. No matter how quickly your balance declines over time, you are still stuck paying the same rate as when you first started the policy. For example, someone taking out a $100,000 mortgage purchases the life insurance plan. They pay a large monthly premium for the protection. Twenty years later, when they only owe $15,000 on the mortgage, if the person dies, the insurance company only has to pay out the $15,000. And it goes directly to the Mortgage Company even though you paid the $100,000 coverage fee for 20 years. In other words if you take this option you better choose to die very quickly to make the most of this. The best option is to purchase term life insurance for $100,000. This will result in a lower monthly cost than the bank will charge and if you do die 20 years later your estate gets the $85,000 after the balance of the mortgage ($15,000) is paid out. In the first scenario you are paying the bank's insurance policy for them. The same concept applies to any other device such as credit cards, for which you are encouraged to buy coverage for outstanding balances. Sweet for the banks, not for you.

Whole Life, Cash Value and Universal Insurance

Over 79% of all North American adults believe that life insurance is too complicated, confusing and expensive. The result is people are often being taken advantage of by unscrupulous insurance companies or agents, or that consumers simply decide not to invest in proper insurance. It is estimated that over 100 million adults have no life insurance or insufficient coverage. As we mentioned before, life insurance should only be purchased for protection. It is *not* an investment. That's why we haven't dealt with insurance in the investment section of the book. Tens of millions of North Americans are buying Whole Life, Cash Value or Universal insurance as an investment, and in our opinion, it is one of the greatest Wealth Robbers.

Let's revisit the basics. The purpose of life insurance is *protection* in the event of catastrophe. The purpose of an investment is to maximize *wealth*. So, your goal should be to obtain the maximum life protection (Term insurance) at a competitive price, with a policy that provides the option to increase should your needs grow, while simultaneously investing as much money per month as possible in the best investment vehicles.

Two additional drawbacks to Whole Life insurance:
1. If you die, your survivors cannot collect both the face amount and the cash value of your policy. Most consumers are unaware

of the fact that they can only collect the cash value component of their policies while they are alive. Your beneficiary will get the face value of the policy but not the accumulated cash portion. If, for example, you buy a policy with a face amount of $200,000 and then accumulate cash values of $39,000 your family will only get the $200,000 face value if you die. They will not get the $39,000. All of your hard earned payments over the years have just gone out the window.

2. You must pay to borrow your own money. One of the main selling points of 'cash value' policies is the ability to borrow against your policy. But, most consumers are not aware that they will have to pay interest to borrow their money. To add insult to injury, if you the policy holder should die prior to paying back the loan in full, the outstanding amount, of *your* money, will be deducted from the death benefit your beneficiary receives!

In short, never buy Whole Life, Cash Value or Universal insurance. Instead, **buy Term insurance** and then invest the money you save in investment vehicles such as IRAs and in creating Multiple Sources of Income.

Term Life Insurance

Remember when you are buying this that it is tied to your needs at different periods in your life. A newlywed couples' needs are not as great as they are a few years later when they have children and a mortgage. Then, later on in life when the mortgage is paid off and the kids have left home, your needs are again different. You do not need to pay for as much coverage. Of course, these events happen at different ages to different people. You may not need insurance after age 35 while others may need full coverage until they are 70. You are better off dedicating that extra money to investments either in financial vehicles or your own business ventures. Do not pay for what you do not need.

How Much Life Insurance Do I Need?

To determine your life insurance needs, do some simple calculations.

Step 1: Determine how much family income you need each year to maintain your current life-style.

Step 2: Multiply the required annual family income by ten. The ten represents a ten per cent annual rate of return achieved by investing the insurance settlement.

For instance, if your family requires $50,000 per year to maintain your current life-style, then you would do the following calculation: $50,000 × 10 = $500,000. Thus your family would require $500,000 of term life insurance coverage.

When buying insurance for your spouse, buy it as a rider on your own policy rather then as a separate policy. You will get more coverage cheaper. Do not buy insurance on the children; add a $5,000 per child burial costs rider to your own insurance. Again, insurance is not an investment.

Disability Insurance

Purchasing some form of disability insurance is a good idea to provide for the entire family should the breadwinner become permanently disabled. Our advice is be a short-term self-insurer and buy only long-term disability insurance. As we discussed earlier, it is a very good idea to have a minimum of a three-month emergency fund (longer is even better). Placing money into a sound investment plan will pay greater long-term benefits than dumping it into a short-term disability insurance policy. The premiums for long-term disability insurance can be greatly reduced by increasing the standard waiting period from three months to six months. The waiting period is similar to a deductible; it is the amount of time you must be disabled and unable to work before the insurance takes effect. If you become temporarily disabled you will not suddenly lose everything. If you are injured on the job, your employer's or state compensation insurance should cover you; you may have unemployment insurance as an option plus the emergency fund is there if you need it.

Tips to Buying and Paying Off Your Mortgage

There are many places to obtain a mortgage so the first rule is to shop around until you get the best deal. If you have a troubled credit history then you may need to find someone like a family member to co-sign the loan. As confusing as some of the offers may seem, you really need to work through the math in order to get the best deal. A mortgage broker *may* help you find a better deal than you could on your own though there will be a cost. As we saw in the sub-prime meltdown, there are plenty of unscrupulous lenders around who will get you into a loan you ultimately won't be able to afford. So, make sure you get and check the references from any broker first. Then get a lawyer to check the deal for you. It's worth the price. A dodgy broker may simply steer you to a friend of his with a higher rate. The broker gets a kickback and you lose to both of them.

Owing to the competition for mortgages, many lenders compete by offering deals that seem enticing but benefit them more than you in the long run. For example, you may be offered a cash incentive to move or open a new mortgage. It sounds great until you realize that the interest rate attached to it will cost you much more than they will give you. Similarly with tiered rates, although the first year is quite cheap it does not justify the high costs of the succeeding years. So, beware of the dazzling come-ons.

Let's start with the basics. Many people see the goal as paying the lowest possible amount per month and when starting out as a homeowner that is certainly a prime consideration. There are always extra expenses that you have not counted on such as higher than expected closing costs, moving fees, the need to buy new furniture, updating the plumbing, repainting, redecorating, etc. And, you do not want to be a slave to your home's costs. Some lenders will allow you to borrow a little extra to accommodate these items and roll it into the cost of the mortgage. You do want a low interest rate; just make sure that there are no strings or hidden costs attached. Shopping from lender to lender, or even threatening to, may save as much as a whole point of interest. This can save you thousands of dollars. You may also avoid extra fees such as account setup charges simply by threatening to go elsewhere. Always negotiate!

If your lender does not offer you the option of paying the mortgage every two weeks, find another lender. What this does is it makes you pay an extra two installments every year. If you pay once a month, for example, there are 12 full payments. Paying every two weeks means that you will make 26 half payments, or 13 full payments per year. If you get paid every two weeks, you will never notice this and save thousands of dollars as a result.

Example:
Amount borrowed $100,000 at seven per cent interest rate over 25 years.

Monthly payment option:
$700.42 (principal and interest) × 12 × 25 years = $210,126
Total interest paid = $110,126.

Every two weeks payment option:
$350.21 (principal and interest) × 26 × 20.3 years = $184,840.83
Total interest paid = $84,840.83

Interest saved by paying every two weeks: $25,285.17

Note: Do not be fooled by the difference in "bi-weekly" and "bi-monthly" payments. The latter simply allows you to pay twice each month. A friend thought she was getting the benefit of the bi-weekly payment but actually saved absolutely nothing. We switched brokers for her at renewal time.

Now, if you are in a position to pay just a little more than necessary on each payment you will save even more. Let's say your bi-weekly mortgage cost is $350.21 and even after considering all the other costs such as electricity, telephone, taxes, cable, insurance, etc., you could afford to pay an additional $35 per bi-weekly payment on your mortgage (thus your bi-weekly payment would be $385.21). This extra $70 per month will save you thousands of dollars in interest.

Example:
Amount borrowed: $100,000 at seven per cent interest over 25 years.

Bi-weekly payment option:
$385.21 (principal and interest) × 26 × 16.10 years

= $161,248.90
Interest paid = $61,248.90

Interest saved by paying an additional $35 every two weeks:
Another $23,591.93
And the mortgage is paid off in only 16 years, one month!

Remember where we started: Paying the minimum once a month would cost $210,126. These two small steps have just saved you $48,878 AND eight years, 11 months of payments!

Perhaps you can afford more than $70 per month in additional payments. Make the higher payment and watch the term decrease. One other thing. Some people like the option of paying a lump sum once a year on the principal. If that payment is timed to the receipt of an annual bonus for example, it works well. For most people other expenses arise – vacations, appliance breakdowns etc. – and the payment disappears. A few extra dollars per payment is easier to budget and more like to happen.

Consider this: Many people do not buy a home until they are in their 30s. Or, you may not be able to move up to your dream home until you are in your 40s or even later. If you then take out a 25 – 30 year mortgage in order to keep the payments low, you will have the albatross of a large monthly payment hanging around you at the point you want to take early or even full retirement. In fact, this alone may force you to work five or ten years longer than you really want.

We cannot escape the feeling deep down that when governments allow you to deduct the cost of a mortgage from your taxes it is an example of the government doing a massive favor for the banking industry, because a long-term mortgage does not help anyone but them. True, this does allow you to buy a bigger, more expensive home than you might otherwise be able to afford, but at what cost? What if you are out of work for an extended period? What if you want to retire early? Make your payments, build up your equity and use that to move up. We can think of a much better beneficiary for your money and that is you!

Alan writes: "When I bought my first house I was very lucky

in that the mortgage rates were just starting to come down from a historic high point. I was able to put down two thirds of the house price in cash from my savings over the previous three years. The remaining $150,000 was financed at 14 per cent for a one-year term. I chose the year term because going into a home for the first time I knew there would be some initial unexpected expenses to cover. I did not want any surprises if rates went up again after six months. I was reasonably sure, however, that the rates were going to come down within the year and this was the cheapest possible rate. A five-year term would have been almost 16 per cent at the time. The monthly cost was $1,760.81. I voluntarily raised the amount by $30 each payment to pay off a little bit of the principal. My mortgage balance at the end of the year was $148,852.11.

"When it was time to renew for a six-month period the rate had dropped to 12.25 per cent and I was able to negotiate that down to 11.75 per cent because I had always made my payments promptly. The new monthly cost was $1,563.91. I agreed to the term but insisted on keeping the payments the same as I had already built the $1,790.81 into my budgeting and in fact added another $25 per payment, thus making my new monthly payment $1,815.81. This is called making "accelerated payments" and the nice lady in charge of the loan department smiled kindly at me and congratulated me for my discipline. At this point I started paying off $251.90 per month from the principal. After 18 months my mortgage balance was $146,438.46.

"Six months later the rate was ten per cent which I negotiated to 9.75 per cent and I added another $50 to my monthly payment making it $1,865.81

"I was now paying $731.47 per month towards the principal. During this period I had managed to sell a broadcast of an old program to a foreign country for a license fee, my half of which was an unbudgeted $7,610. As I was not expecting this money and it happened to arrive just a few weeks before my renewal, I turned $7,500 (the balance went to purchase an excellent bottle of wine) over to my loan manager. My mortgage balance after 30 months was $130,160.39.

"By the time of the next renewal, the rates had dropped to eight per cent and my loan manager was starting to eye me suspiciously whenever I walked into the bank. In the meantime, I had read about a new payment option, that being the bi-weekly payment which we discussed above. This time I told her I was going to celebrate the fact that business was going very well and instead of keeping my payment at $1,865.81, I was going to change the frequency of payments and increase the monthly amount. I had decided to make bi-weekly payments of $1,000. This may seem a little fantastic to some people so, in fairness I should mention that as I was actively working in the music industry. Thus, my entertainment overhead was nonexistent. I was always being invited to show openings, movie premieres and concerts and plied with seemingly endless amounts of alcohol and meals. Fortunately, I have a low tolerance for alcohol so I never lost my head to the demon as so many in that business do. The point is that all of my socializing, partying and travelling interests were being paid by other companies so that whatever fees I charged or earned had no place else to go but to eliminate my mortgage and into my retirement savings plans.

This pattern continued wherein interest rates declined and my loan manager did everything she could think of to avoid me. My last interest rate was six per cent and after a few years of paying every two weeks and keeping bi-weekly payments at $1,000, only $295.48 per bi-weekly payment was interest while fully $1,409.04 was going towards the principal every month. Very much to the chagrin of my loan manager I paid off my "25-year" mortgage in just under ten years. Of all the things I could do with my time, energy and money, making me richer seemed the best option."

It is really easy to spend money. Our whole economic system is based on providing the shortest, easiest path between your check book and someone else's pocket. We are bombarded daily by very sophisticated advertising designed to convince you, that you will be better, look better or feel better if only you purchase certain products or services. Wealthy people do not buy into those myths. You shouldn't either!

Wealth is largely a result of habit.

– Jack Astor

Reading this chapter you should have learned two things. First, when you look very carefully at how you spend every dollar, you will usually find that you can easily live without many things you take for granted. Secondly, the better educated you become as a consumer, the more money you will keep in your own bank account. Getting as much value as you can for the least amount of money is a game and, after a short while, it starts to become fun. This chapter covers some of the basics in keeping more of your money in your own pocket. The next step is to start to appreciate the real value of the assets you already have and use them to further your goals.

Let's take a couple of seconds to review the key points covered in this chapter.

1. What can I do to behave in a frugal fashion, delaying instant gratification?
2. What is the difference between income and wealth?
3. What insights have I gained as a result of completing the Financial Freedom Indicator?
4. How would I define "budgeting?"
5. How do I feel about creating a budget and sticking to it?
6. What do I need to do to ensure that I stay on budget?
7. What have I learned about my spending habits after completing the Monthly Money Monitor?
8. What are the areas where I have to reduce my spending?
9. How will I use my Financial Snapshot to achieve my goals?
10. Which methods of "Stretching a Dollar" will I adopt as a new behavior?
11. What will I do to ensure that I avoid being financially trapped by Wealth Robbers?

5

THE BEHAVIOR OF LEVERAGING
Earning More with Less

Trinidad is a beautiful country just off the northern tip of South America. In the many times we have been there we do not remember the temperature dipping below 80 degrees. We had been invited by the country's government to shoot a television show dedicated to raising self-esteem in teenagers. Our excellent local production company partner had arranged to put us in a five-star hotel overlooking the capital city, Port of Spain.

Lingering over a dinner one night, we were discussing the logistics of getting this book out of our heads and into print. Looking around at the palm trees and bougainvillea bushes it started to seem like a very good idea to relocate our "office" southward. On the back of a napkin we drafted our goal – a five star resort on a Caribbean island for four nonconsecutive weeks, and it should be all-inclusive so that we can focus all our energies on writing. With the goal now in hand we had several options. We could pick a resort, pull out our respective plastic cards and enjoy the fact that, as we were going to be working most of the time, the trip would be tax deductible. After further discussion and another round of Carib beer, we decided we needed to get a little more creative. What we really wanted was for a resort to give us the trips for free.

So what scenario could we possibly devise as leverage for a resort to see life the way we did? It was what can only be described as a three Carib problem. Eventually, Denis remembered meeting the then head of training for the Sandals Resorts International chain of hotels after delivering an executive level seminar in Jamaica. One of the most impressive and successful resort chains in the world, Sandals is a leader in customer service and believes in the benefits of regular employee training.

We got in touch with Sandals and, calling on our combined 25 years of training experience, agreed that in exchange for a one-day staff customer service workshop, they would give us two rooms in which we could work on our book for a week or two. Through their contacts with other luxury resorts in the Caribbean, a similar arrangement was set up for other weeks of training and writing. The resorts were so pleased with the results of the training that in each case our rooms were upgraded to luxury suites. What we had done was leverage our existing skills to meet our stated goal in a way that left both parties completely satisfied. Each property gave us unsolicited letters of praise which we have been able to leverage for more business at other hotels around the world over the past year. And, in the process, we identified some new business opportunities. Now we just need to find a lever for the Carib Brewery.

There are many obstacles to becoming wealthy, but if you use the power of leveraging you stand an excellent chance of succeeding. To fully tap into the power of wealth leveraging you need to understand how to make your own levers more effective. One of the best ways to increase the power of your leverage is to acquire more knowledge and then combine that knowledge with the development of your skills. In this chapter we will share with you the three ways in which you can leverage your day-to-day behaviors to generate wealth.

The most common method of leveraging is called the job. In this case what we are leveraging is our time, energy and effort in return for an hourly rate or salary. Our first goal is to connect you with your ideal job. This is one where you are not only paid well but in which you also feel a sense of connectedness to the work. A sense of passion for a job will raise overall satisfaction and help you become more productive. The greater a person's productivity, the greater the chances for more compensation. When an employer assesses the real value of an employee, they are considering a combination of 26 typical characteristics (please see page 122). In this section we will show you how to fatten your bank accounts by understanding these characteristics. The more of these you possess, the greater your market value as an employee.

Free Agent

If you choose to be an employee because of security, social or other reasons you should seriously consider yourself as a free agent. Just as in sports, where the athletes "lease" themselves (their talent, skills and branding) to the highest bidder for the duration of a contract, you should consider leasing your mind, experience, skills and network to the highest bidding employer. The reality is that no organization can really offer you true job security. Instead, as a free agent, investing in your own personal growth and career development, you become your best form of employment security.

The second form of wealth leverage is called investing. In this case we are leveraging money to make more money. The ideal scenario is for a person to live within their means AND to have a minimum surplus of ten per cent. Such a fund allows you to move quickly towards wealth generation. Most people think that it takes a tremendous amount of money to become a millionaire. This is not true. Take, for example, an individual working in a minimum wage job who has very limited funds. If this person were to save $100 per month and invest it wisely, he would amass a surprising amount of money over his working lifetime. Beginning at age 21, saving $25 per week with a ten per cent rate of return on the investment would generate $1,041,396 by the time he turns 65! Once the savings habit is established it is much easier to put aside additional funds. After a few years, with a raise in pay, our friend may start putting away $50 per week. All of a sudden he has a very respectable portfolio and independence.

The third and least common, yet most powerful, form of

wealth leverage is called Multiple Sources of Income. MSI results from a person creating his or her own business on a full-time basis or supplementing a full-time job with a part-time business often based on a hobby. Research indicates that 74 per cent of all self-made millionaires derive their income from self-owned businesses. In this form of leveraging, we are incorporating unique ideas plus creativity for wealth generation.

MODELS OF LEVERAGING

Typical Time and Effort Leveraging: The Job

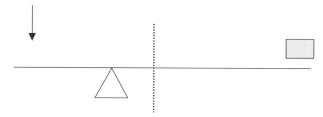

Typical Money Leveraging: Investing

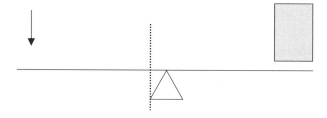

Typical Creativity Leveraging: Multiple Sources of Income

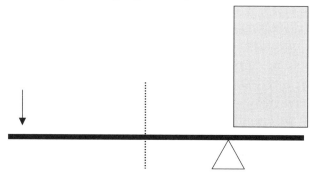

> There is no security on earth. Only opportunity.
>
> – General Douglas MacArthur

The above diagrams depict the power of leveraging. The key is to remember to maximize your personal leverage by adding to your skills and knowledge base while focusing on money-making attitudes and behaviors.

Alan relates the story of Len. "Len is an extremely bright, personable man with a great education and a voracious appetite for books devoted to psychology and learning. He is a trainer by profession, working for a large company. When that company recently merged with another, his job became redundant and was to be terminated in three months. During that time he still had to show up every day but there were no expectations placed upon him. When I asked him how he filled his day he replied that he spent most of his time reading. That is, without question, a worthwhile pursuit, though I thought his main goal should be to find another source of income be it a new job or setting up a new business. I asked him if his desk came equipped with a phone and if he had a computer with Internet access to which he replied, 'yes.' 'Well then why aren't you spending your days building your new career or looking for a new job?' I asked in puzzlement. 'I do not think my boss would really approve' came the reply. 'What can she do; fire you? They have already done that. I don't see what you have to lose' said the cynic. 'Firstly, I am not sure it is really fair to the company who are, after all, still paying me and secondly, if my boss did not like it she may refuse to give me a good letter of recommendation.' 'Okay, then how about this scenario: You approach your boss and suggest to her that they utilize some of the expensive multimedia equipment they have on premises to tape you performing a training seminar. There would be no direct cost to them and they would then have a tape they could play for years at no cost. Meanwhile you bring the in-house editor a case of beer and ask him to spend an hour or two customizing the opening of the tape for you and then use it as a demo of your training abilities. It may be the leverage you need to land a new job or, when you are ready, to launch your career as an independent trainer.' 'I am not sure the company would go for that either' he replied.

"At this point I stopped the conversation because I could sense his unwillingness to take any chances with his main source of income. And I respect this. For all his positive attributes, the one quality Len lacks is the 'self-starter' trait common to all entrepreneurs. That is a crucial thing to know about yourself. He can, instead, focus his energies on saving and building a powerful investment portfolio, which will, if he's diligent, allow him to take an early retirement. He should still read Section C of this book in case his situation changes in the future. It is possible that one day he will gain more confidence in his abilities and feel comfortable pursuing an independent route, or he may find himself frustrated with his job and be forced to take an independent step."

Len represents a very common mindset. Our advice is to look carefully at yourself to see if this one is common to you. If that is the case, there is nothing wrong with you and you are in good company. For now, save yourself the lost sleep. Do not even go down the independent route at this point in your life. The benefits do not equal the costs. Concentrate on frugality and building a savings or investment plan.

Contrast that situation with Sabena, a young, high-energy, personable host we met at a broadcasting convention in Los Angeles a few years ago. She was anxious to break into the business and had volunteered her time to the company that had us on a retainer.

Occasionally, one of us would get an idea that would raise our client's profile. By the time we had expressed the full idea to the other, Sabena had left to find the exact person necessary to execute the plan. Almost everyone attending the convention was aware of her by the time it was over and were hugely impressed with her ability to network. Her only limitation was that she did not have an extensive formal education or much knowledge of the broadcasting field. Our advice to her was to read a selection of books we suggested. Then we helped her choose and enrol in a community college level-broadcasting course. She was admitted and beginning the readings by the end of that week. Before she had finished the last part of the course, a major radio chain had swept her up. In this case a good basic knowledge of the industry combined with her genuine enthusiasm outstripped the need for a diploma. The story, however, does not end there. After about 18 months of practical, on-the-job experience, she left to help set up a consulting business with some associates. She is currently living her dream and is in control of her destiny as anyone can be. Oh, yes, she is making great money and investing it wisely. She will not be among those who retire below the poverty line.

In this chapter we want to encourage the reader to move through the process of becoming financially independent using very small steps, emphasizing that new moves be taken only when they are comfortable with the previous step and feeling secure enough to move to the next. This does not mean that progress has to necessarily be slow. The reader can walk up the ladder as quickly or slowly as they want, as long as he or she steps on every rung. We recognize that for many of you some of these new behaviors and strategies are intimidating. For this reason we present the steps and let you proceed at your own comfort level.

At first we suggest you maintain the security of your primary jobs while devoting portions of your income for investments in new wealth creation. The first and easiest investments are the traditional ones: Mutual and Index funds, and Bonds and Savings Certificates. Once this new savings routine is established, we encourage you to take these gains or additional funds to invest in a small business of your own. This can be accomplished initially, on a part-time basis without jeopardizing the primary income. If the first attempt at a small business is unsuccessful, the idea is to take the learning from that experience and apply it to another idea. Ultimately, the small business should grow to become the primary source of income.

FOUR PERSONAL ASSETS TO INVEST, NOT SPEND

Every person possesses some degree of the following four personal assets.

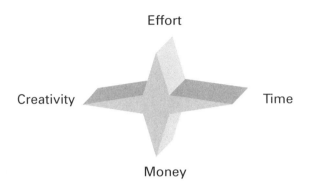

The problem is that most people take these for granted and do not truly see them as assets. Money Minimizers often spend time frivolously. A Money Magnet values the precious asset called time and consciously decides in which activities he or she wishes to invest their time. The difference is that if you see something as an asset you will take very good care of it. You will also expect to receive a certain return on investment. For example, if you owned a three-million-dollar racehorse, you wouldn't hitch it to the back of a plough and work it to death tilling the fields. You would not let the horse smoke or drink booze. You are your most valuable asset, so take very good care of yourself and do not undersell yourself. Bet money on your own horse, not on someone else's. The goal is to maximize the return on investment, for every investment.

WEALTH LEVERAGING BEHAVIORS ON THE JOB

To our way of thinking these are the five characteristics of the ideal job.

1. High income.
2. Great opportunity to learn about management of money, self and others.
3. Ongoing networking with wealthy people.
4. Fun and companionship.
5. Exposure to various opportunities for Multiple Sources of Income.

Financial Decision Tree

For most people, a job is the easiest way of earning an income. With a proper job, if you adopt the wealth-building behaviors we have already discussed, you will be well on your way to a comfortable retirement. A job also gives you a base from which to begin work on other sources of income such as part-time jobs and new businesses which we will discuss in Section C. So, the first step is to get a job or, perhaps, apply for a more appropriate, higher paying job.

From Denis' years of experience working with employers seeking to hire the right staff, here are some of the key elements that influence whether a candidate is successful in landing or progressing in a job. This list assumes that you already have the basic qualifications and skills required for the job and that punctuality and appropriate clothing are not issues of concern.

Understand the Employer's Point of View

Once again, tap into the power of Reality Immersion by putting yourself in the employer's shoes. Understand the macro view of the company and the impact of a specific job. Analyze the job and determine which of the following 26 values are required to perform at the peak level. Then ask yourself which of the values you possess. To learn more about how employers think, read books and articles on the subject of hiring staff (see Appendix 1). To learn more about how Denis and Alan can help a company hire and retain exceptional employees please check out our website: www.abcguys.com.

The Employment Leverage Indicator

Instructions: Circle the number which comes closest to representing how true the statement is for you right now (a rating of one would represent never true, while a rating of five would represent always true).

Statement	Ranking
I have a proven ability in increasing sales for my employer.	1 2 3 4 5
I have demonstrated the ability to cut costs.	1 2 3 4 5
I possess the skills and knowledge to make almost any situation look better.	1 2 3 4 5
I find ways to accomplish tasks faster without compromising quality.	1 2 3 4 5
I know many low-cost, high-impact ways to expand business.	1 2 3 4 5
I am a professional and my actions place my employer in a favorable light.	1 2 3 4 5
I am a constant source of timely, relevant job-related information.	1 2 3 4 5
I make a direct, positive impact on the bottom-line.	1 2 3 4 5
I have experience opening new territories.	1 2 3 4 5
I can stabilize a situation by diversifying the risks.	1 2 3 4 5
I know how to cut labor costs without it negatively affecting productivity and morale.	1 2 3 4 5

I know how to tap into government support.	1 2 3 4 5
I enjoy turning around negative situations.	1 2 3 4 5
I enjoy the challenge of creating and maintaining a competitive advantage.	1 2 3 4 5
I can contribute to increased sales by modifying the packaging.	1 2 3 4 5
I can help the company avoid potential problems.	1 2 3 4 5
I am successful at organizing complex projects.	1 2 3 4 5
I create systems that expedite workflow.	1 2 3 4 5
I consistently provide or obtain faster and more economical deliveries.	1 2 3 4 5
I can find productive uses for old and discarded items.	1 2 3 4 5
I can inspire a team of people to deliver peak performance.	1 2 3 4 5
I can reduce the amount of corporate taxes payable.	1 2 3 4 5
I am able to quickly increase market shares.	1 2 3 4 5
I have a proven track record of reducing the cost of inventories.	1 2 3 4 5
I can maximize the ROI (Return on Investment) on Information Technology systems.	1 2 3 4 5
I can create an expanding, loyal client base.	1 2 3 4 5

Interpretation: A score of five in any statement demonstrates an area of strength that is highly valued by today's employers.

Questions to consider:
1. Into which areas should I focus my energies to increase my on-the-job performance?
2. What is the best way to proceed to enhance my job performance?
3. Does my current job require all of my talents?
4. Should I consider finding a new job that would more fully utilize my talents so that I can receive a higher wage?
5. What other jobs or opportunities should I investigate further?
6. Is my boss or prospective employer aware that I have these skills?

Top Ten Places Employers Search for New Employees

1. Promote from Within

According to Hertzberg's theory of motivation, giving recognition to employees ranks as one of the highest motivators. With that in mind many employers consider the first source of recruitment to be their existing staff through a promote-from-within policy. Savvy employers recognize the fact that bypassing existing employees for promotional consideration is a sure-fire way to reduce morale and productivity and increase the level of staff turnover. An Employer of Choice deliberately promotes from within as a strategy to retain the best employees. The opportunity is to find out who these employers are and get a job with them.

2. Employee Referrals

Many employers will turn to trusted employees to get their advice and assistance in referring their friends and acquaintances to apply for vacant positions. The advantages of this method are manyfold. The referred individual is more apt to have a realistic expectation of the job and the company because the employee will have related both the benefits and pitfalls of working for the firm. In addition, the referring employee does not want to lose face, thus they are likely only to recommend someone who can do the job well over the long term. The key here is to be networked with the type of people that can refer you to their employer.

3. On-line Recruitment

In March 2008 there were over one billion Internet users. Forty-two per cent of these have used the Net as part of their job search activities. (Source: www.monster.com)

Unfolding at lightning speed is a cyberworld filled with great opportunities to both earn and learn more than ever before. The Internet has become one of the preferred sources of recruiting employees for many companies. The Net has become such a popular place to seek employment that by January 2008 there were more than 500 million registered resumes on-line. Ninety-four per cent of all post-secondary American graduates were using the Net as part of their job search. Denis predicts that by the end of 2008, 95 per cent of all companies with ten or more employees will adopt on-line recruitment as part of their overall recruiting strategy. Companies use two primary methods of on-line recruiting: company website and on-line recruitment portals. The first method is when the company places its employment opportunities in the career or job section of its web page. If the job seeker clicks on the site they can review the various job opportunities, find out more about the job and the company and in most cases even apply for the job on-line.

The second method is by going through a third party on-line recruiting portal. This is where the third-party firm goes on-line and advertises all of the job offers from their clients. Usually, there is no cost for the job seeker to view the opportunities or to apply. The employers, who are the portal's clients, pay the costs. The following are the URLs of some of the largest and better-known on-line recruitment portals.

www.monster.com
www.careers.yahoo.com
www.ecruiter.com
www.hotjobs.com
www.jobshark.com
www.workopolis.com

The key to tapping into this fantastic global pool of employment opportunities is to get on-line at home, the local library or a cybercafe, use your favorite search engine and, for starters, check out the six portals listed. The generic portals noted, in our experience, treat clients professionally and with respect. Generic means that they are not industry or country-specific. They advertise job openings virtually around the world ranging from entry level to executive and from the public to the private sector. They are all established and are seen as professional by both employers and job seekers. Remember that on the better sites, the job seeker does not need to pay a fee.

4. Private Employment Agencies

Employers often contract out the function of staff selection to a professional employment agency that will be responsible for the placement of the advertisement and pre-screening of applicants. In some cases, the agency will even conduct the first interview. In most cases a representative of the company doing the hiring conducts the final interview. Usually, there is no cost incurred by the job seeker. The company covers the agency's fees. Another valuable service provided by employment agencies is executive search or head hunting, as the practice is commonly known. Executive search professionals have exhaustive lists of people, both unemployed and underemployed, from which to draw for selection purposes. They will often contact the passive job seeker and describe the job opportunity to them. In other words, they pro-actively seek out potential applicants rather than just wait by the telephone for someone to respond to an advertisement. The best way to be approached by an employment agency when the right opportunity arises is to be known by the agency through personal contact and by maintaining an up-to-date resume with them.

5. Walk-ins

Many employers in the retail and service sector post "Help Wanted" signs in their windows to attract the attention of potential job seekers who pass by.

Sophia, a successful entrepreneur and ladies high-fashion boutique owner says that her number-one source for finding great sales staff is through walk-ins. Because of a very exclusive and limited client base, Sophia will ask any walk-in this all-important question: "When did you last purchase something here?" The idea behind this question is that a potential salesperson who has shopped at Sofia's boutique is more likely to be of a similar mind-set and have more things in common with Sofia's client base. Thus she will be a more successful salesperson.

Before walking in off the street to apply for the job, applicants should invest the time to research the company and determine the opportunities and challenges that face the business and how it will benefit most from the job seekers' skills and abilities. After the research is complete, approach the company by setting up a brief information interview and/or drop off your resume.

6. Newspapers

One of the most widely used sources of recruitment is a newspaper advertisement in the Employment Opportunities or Career section. One caution is to think twice about responding to "blind" advertisements. These are ones in which the advertiser fails to identify itself and asks you to respond to a box number. You may not like the employer when you find out who it is and it prevents you from customizing your resume to a company's needs. Turning the tables, you can try placing your own advertisement in the middle of the employment ones. Human Resources people are reading these pages and you will stand out with a proper advertisement. Obviously, the potential income of the job you are seeking has to be high enough to warrant the upfront expense.

7. Professional Associations

Professional associations provide a fertile ground for employers seeking large pools of talent in a specific area. The key to capitalising on this source is what we call the Four Cs:

Conventions and Conferences. Most employers realize that the best people have jobs or are job-hunting for only a short period of time. A great place to find these individuals is at conventions and conferences. For example, to find an engineer, an employer will often go to an Engineer Society's annual conference and network with the movers and shakers in the industry to find out who is looking for a career change.

The key is to be one of those people who attend conferences and conventions with the aim of constantly upgrading your skills, knowledge and network base. In our estimation, potential employers will see you as the cream of the crop.

Committees. Another way to use professional associations as a source for job opportunities is to become very involved in several committees within the association. This type of networking will open many doors to finding potential employers seeking your specific qualifications.

Circulations. Most professional associations produce circulations, i.e. newsletters, bulletins, etc., which are distributed on a regular basis to all members. These publications provide employers an excellent vehicle for placing recruiting advertisements.

8. Open House

Open Houses are a recruiting method, which have been successfully used by many companies. Usually, there is an advertisement or poster that outlines the particulars of the Open House. For example, in real estate, a Century 21 real estate broker hosts an Open House at his or her office (or some other convenient location), where they showcases career opportunities within the real estate industry and their specific organization.

An Open House provides an excellent non-threatening opportunity to learn more about that particular industry. As a result, if someone is excited about a career opportunity in real estate, they can then go through the application process. Some of the industries that commonly use this source of recruiting are insurance companies, financial institutions, automotive sales and retailers.

9. Volunteer Associations

A new source for potential staff on which employers are now starting to focus more attention is volunteer associations. Let's say that a company is looking for a supervisor and is experiencing a difficult time finding the ideal person. A non-traditional place to find someone with these talents is a volunteer association. For instance, the person who is going to head up the telemarketing fund-raising campaign for the local Heart Foundation will be accountable for many things, such as organizing and co-ordinating the campaign and revving up dozens of volunteers to be productively effective in achieving the campaign goals. This person usually possesses excellent interpersonal and motivational skills and natural leadership qualities.

One of the challenges of supervising a group of volunteers is that these people work very hard without drawing a paycheck, so you can't motivate them with financial incentive or the fear of getting fired. Nevertheless, an effective fund-raising captain will lead his or her team through numerous obstacles, while achieving a high rate of success. Savvy recruiters understand these principles and actively seek volunteers with positive attitudes and transferable skills. By volunteering you can do something nice by giving back to your community, develop your skills and knowledge and maybe land that ideal job!

10. Competitors, Customers and Suppliers

In the summer of 1982, Denis was the manager of a Pizza Hut franchise and was having what can be categorized as a crummy day. Within a two-hour span, two waitresses and one waiter gave notice (each for personal reasons) that they were leaving by the end of the week. "Faced with this dilemma, I did what any good Pizza Hut manager would do – I went to the local McDonald's restaurant. I placed myself in a strategic location so that I could overlook the activity at the front counter.

"What I saw was a young woman (named Leslie) who was outperforming the other six workers on the line. Leslie had the ability to up-sell more fries, drinks and desserts than half the other staff combined. While her counterparts droned on in an automated voice, "Will there be anything else?" Leslie was busy up-selling her customers in a friendly, natural manner.

After watching her in action for about half-an-hour, including the professional way in which she dealt with a sexual advance from an intoxicated customer, I was convinced she possessed the necessary attributes to be a successful waitress at my restaurant.

"I approached Leslie, introduced myself and asked her how much money she made per hour. She replied '$3.75 per hour' which was minimum wage at the time. I asked her if she would be interested in working for $7 per hour minimum, guaranteed. Her eyes enlarged substantially, then she leaned over and gasped, 'Is this legal?' I replied that not only was it legal, but it could also provide a job that was more enjoyable than the one she was currently doing.

"I explained my position, my predicament and the opportunity I was offering her. She asked how she could capitalise on the job offer to which I replied: 'Grab your coat, leap over this counter and let's get to work!' Her reply was a surprise: 'I'm sorry, Mr. Cauvier, I will not be able to take you up on your offer unless I could give my employer two weeks notice.' Hearing this, I considered presenting her with the ultimatum, 'Take my offer now, or never' but decided against such a quick reaction, because I felt that if she was going to pay her employer the courtesy of giving notice, she would probably never leave me in a bind either. This was a great illustration of someone with the right attitude.

"We agreed that she would start working in two weeks from that date. Asking if there was anything else she could do for me, I replied, 'Is there anyone else here that I should be looking at?' She suggested I observe the young lady at the take-out window and survey the cooking area. 'You can't be serious, not the burger flipper!' I replied. 'Take several moments and just watch these people, I think you'll be impressed,' she added. The young woman at the take-out window had a tremendous way of dealing with the customers and was very efficient, while the cook at the back was a true leader. He encouraged team support and maintained the pace of the entire kitchen. His people skills were substantially greater than his years would suggest. All three made the job switch.

"Four years later, when I had the opportunity to visit that Pizza Hut outlet, I learned that the two women servers were leaders in inside sales and the young man had moved on to a senior management position within the company."

The point we are making is: While at work deliver at your best performance; it makes you most attractive as a key employee to your employer, your employer's competition and even your customers, all of whom will occasionally need to hire someone. That next someone could be you.

Getting the right job is like closing a big deal. In order to be successful it often requires specific skills. One of the most important skills in finding and getting that ideal job is the ability to market and sell yourself.

Marketing yourself is required if you want potential employers to become aware that you exist. In business a good marketer uses various tools to create both awareness and a favorable impression in the minds of the target market. Promotions, Public Relations,

Publicity and Advertising are tools that serve this purpose. Even if the marketer is successful in creating a favorable state of mind there is no guarantee that the intended buyer will buy.

The second skill is critical in order to capitalise on the marketer's efforts. This skill is selling. With effective sales skills the business can develop a relationship with the prospective buyer, uncover their unique requirements that are satisfied by the product or service offering, overcome any objections, negotiate the best terms possible and finally close the deal.

When seeking your ideal job you need to use these two critical skills. First, to be seen by the right employers and then to get the right job under the right conditions (pay, benefits, training and development opportunities). Denis has an example of how this type of thinking can pay off.

"Several years ago, a young woman approached me after a seminar to provide her with some assistance in approaching a specific company for a job she wanted to apply for. She was about to graduate from a two-year drafting course and had learned through her research that the most successful architectural firm in the city was looking to hire two junior draft people. She learned that the competition for the positions would be very high, but despite her lack of formal job experience she was going to try her best to get the job. I suggested that she try to learn more about the business issues and challenges that confronted the firm and how she could be part of the solution.

"After several days of research she reported back to me that the new Chief Executive Officer wanted to instill a sales and customer service mindset throughout the entire firm. Armed with this information, I suggested she make some modifications to her resume and portfolio. What we came up with was to take her resume and reprint it out on 'Blueprint' paper complete with a legend and drafting symbols. Her new resume was a personal brochure that told the story of her skills, knowledge and formal training but also showcased her talent and creativity. She then wrote her covering letter in the form of a sales letter, which she wrapped around the 'Blueprint' resume. The sales letter identified several specific areas that her skills, knowledge and personality would be of great value to the firm. She then packaged the sales letter and 'Blueprint' resume into a Blueprint packing tube, labelled it 'Blueprints for Your Hiring Success' and couriered it directly to the CEO.

"The CEO was so impressed with the innovative approach that he instructed his Human Resources manager to interview her for the job. During the interview she used a similar approach by converting the interview into more of a sales presentation. Needless to say, she got the job but in addition she also negotiated the highest starting salary for any new graduate in that area." Chapter 6 covers personal selling and negotiating skills in more detail.

The following are 100 Powerful Interviewing Questions from Denis' international best-selling book, *Attracting, Selecting and Retaining GREAT People*. Before going for a job interview read these over and consider your answer to each one. Some employers may ask a few of these questions, while the more thorough may ask all of them. You will be far better off if you have an answer for all of these questions. Your responses should not seem rehearsed but convey the message that you are aware of your strengths and weaknesses and have considered the reasons you want the job for which you are applying. By considering each of these questions you will avoid being caught off guard and using the very unsatisfying "Gee, I don't know" as an answer.

When you are considering your responses to the questions, put yourself in the employer's shoes and imagine the response that he or she would want to hear. You do not want to lie, so if there are some negative aspects to your employment record, now is the time to consider a response that positions the problem in a more favorable light, such as: "That was very unfortunate but it was an excellent learning lesson, one that I think about often". Another thing to avoid, if you have had some problems in the past, is to constantly put the blame on other people. As with most things, taking the higher moral ground will reflect best on you. Which of the two responses do you think will get you farther ahead: "Oh, that only happened because the guy in shipping really had it in for me." Or, "That was unfortunate. It was the result of two different approaches to getting the job done." Show that you can accept the responsibility for certain mistakes. As we said earlier, if you take responsibility and demonstrate that you have learned from the experience, you will look better in the eyes of an employer or a spouse, family or friend.

What Employers Look For

Work Experience

Areas employers will want to cover during the interview:
Earliest jobs, part-time, temporary, full-time positions and career to date.

Sample questions employers ask:

1. Could you describe your career with _____?
2. Tell me about your work experience in general terms, beginning with your job as _____ and leading up to your present job.
3. Tell me about some of your achievements that have been recognized by your superiors.
4. Will you describe your current duties and responsibilities?
5. Would you tell me more specifically about your duties as _____ with _____?
6. What do you feel were some of your most important accomplishments in your job as _____?
7. What are some of the reasons for considering other employment at this time?
8. How would you describe your current or past supervisor? What do you consider to have been his or her major strengths and weaknesses?
9. What are some things your supervisors have complemented you on? What have they criticized?
10. How do you think your current or past supervisor would describe you?
11. What are some of the things you particularly like about your job as_____?
12. What did you not enjoy?
13. What are some things that frustrate you most in your current job?
14. What were some of the setbacks and disappointments you experienced?

15. What were some problems you encountered on your job as _____ and how did you solve them?
16. What is your impression of (former company)?
17. Why did you leave _____?
18. Why are you pursuing a career as a _____?
19. Tell me about your training. What have you done to improve yourself professionally?
20. What do you like least about the job description?
21. Tell me about a sale that was, for all intents and purposes, lost. How did you turn the situation around?
22. Tell me about how you dealt with an angry or frustrated customer.
23. How do you organize yourself for day-to-day activities?
24. Tell me about the problems you face in getting all the facets of your job completed on time.
25. What is the biggest mistake you have made in your career?
26. How does your boss get the best out of you?
27. Tell me about the last time that you really got angry about a management decision.
28. With what types of employees do you get along best?
29. Tell me some of the ways you have seen managers demotivate employees.
30. What have you been most criticized for as an employee?
31. What do you do when there is a decision to be made and no procedure exists?
32. Tell me about a time when someone lost his or her temper at you in a business environment.
33. Tell me about something you started but could not finish.

Things employers look for: Relevance of work
                            Sufficiency of work
                            Skill and competence
                            Adaptability
                            Productivity
                            Motivation

Interpersonal relations
Leadership
Growth and development

Education

Areas employers will want to cover during the interview:
Elementary school, junior and senior high school, college and
university, any specialized training and recent courses.

Sample questions employers ask:

1. I see you went to (school/university). Could you tell me
   about your education there?
2. How would you describe your academic
   accomplishments?
3. Why did you choose (subject) as an area of study?
4. How did you decide to become a (career/job)?
5. What subjects did you enjoy most? Why?
6. What subjects did you find less enjoyable? Why?
7. What were your best subjects at school/university?
   Why?
8. What subjects did you not do quite so well in? Why?
9. Tell me about any additional training or education
   that you have had since you graduated from school/
   university?
10. How do you think that high school/college contributed
    to your overall development?
11. What are your plans for further education?

Things employers look for: Relevance of schooling
Sufficiency of schooling
Intellectual abilities
Versatility
Breadth and depth of knowledge
Level of accomplishment
Motivation, interest
Reaction to authority
Leadership
Team work

Job Knowledge

Areas employers will want to cover during the interview: Candidate's knowledge and expectation of the job.

Sample questions employers ask:

1. I know you do not (or do) have a great deal of information about it, but what is your perception of the job of (job applied for)?
2. I see you have worked as a _____. Would you describe some of your experiences?
3. What problems did you encounter in your position as _____?
4. What qualities do you think it would take to become a successful (job applied for)?
5. What would you say are some of the problems a supervisor has to face?
6. When you consider your skills as a professional _____, what area concerns you most about your ability to _____?
7. How does this job relate to the overall goals of the company?
8. Explain your understanding of this job's responsibilities.
9. If you were hiring someone for this position, what would you be looking for?
10. What do you expect out of this job?
11. Where do you think you could make the biggest contribution to this organization?

Things employers look for: Accuracy of knowledge and realistic job expectations.

Personal Factors and Outside Activities

Areas employers will want to cover during the interview: Special interests and hobbies, civic and community affairs, finances, health and energy and geographical preferences.

Sample questions employers ask:

1. In general, how would you describe yourself?
2. Describe the sort of career path you would like to follow.
3. Tell me about your career goals and what kind of things you are looking for in a job.
4. What are some things in a job that are important to you?
5. What would you say there is about this job you are applying for that is particularly appealing to you?
6. What are some things that might not be so desirable?
7. Earlier we were talking about your accomplishments as a _____. What would you say accounted for that success?
8. How about the other side of the coin? What sort of personal qualities and abilities would you like to see improved in yourself?
9. What traits or qualities do you most admire in a supervisor?
10. What disappointments, setbacks or failures have you had in life?
11. What kind of situations makes you feel tense and nervous?
12. What are your salary expectations coming into this job?
13. Can you describe a difficult obstacle you have had to overcome? How did you handle it?
14. What do you consider to be your greatest achievement? Why?
15. How do you feel about travelling or working overtime?
16. How do you feel about the right to strike for workers in essential services?
17. Tell me about your recreational or leisure time and interests.
18. You seem to be involved in a number of outside activities. Could you tell me about them?

19. I notice you are involved in _____. Would you tell me about that?

20. Besides _____, what do you like to do with your leisure time?

21. What do you like to avoid getting involved in during your spare time?

22. How do you like to spend your vacations?

23. If you had more time, are there any activities that you would like to participate in? Why?

24. How necessary is it to be creative in your job?

25. What do you consider a good day's effort?

26. What special characteristics should I consider about you as a person?

27. When the pressure is on, where does your extra energy come from?

28. How often do you find it necessary to go above and beyond the call of duty?

29. Give me an example of your initiative in a challenging situation.

30. When do customers and fellow employees really try your patience?

31. What do you feel are your personal limitations?

32. How do you rank among your peers?

33. How do you turn things around when the initial impression of you is bad?

34. What business or social situations make you feel awkward?

35. What kinds of rewards are most satisfying to you?

36. What are some of the things you have found especially motivating over the years?

37. What kinds of decisions are most difficult for you?

38. How do you deal with disagreements with others?

39. How important to you is communication and interaction with the staff?

40. How would you describe the ideal job for you?

41. How do you define a successful career?

42. What can you do for us that someone else cannot?

43. What do you see as some of your most pressing development needs?
44. What have you been involved with that you now regret?
45. What have the disappointments of life taught you?

Things employers look for: Vitality
Management of time, energy and money
Maturity and judgment
Intellectual growth
Cultural breadth
Diversity of interests
Social interests
Social skills
Leadership
Basic values and goals
Situational factors

INVESTING

The second form of leveraging for financial gain is through investment. This is where you allow your money to make more money.

So, you work really hard and sacrifice that extra bottle of wine at your favorite restaurant to build a fund for investing. It is very important then that you do not mistakenly make someone else rich in the process. One thing to avoid is the Get Rich Quick scheme as this usually only enriches the seller. Remember the old cliche: If it seems too good to be true, it probably is.

In this section you will find that you do not need a business degree, or to take unnecessary risks, to profit from the stock market. If you have the interest, by all means take courses and immerse yourself in the world of investments. In this book we are trying to acquaint you with the easiest strategies to get you in the game and make your money work for you. In this process you will learn some tried and true methods from self-made millionaires.

Time is on Your Side

The importance of time as it relates to investments is paramount. It is one of the most critical elements in your creation of extraordinary wealth. Action precedes money-making success, procrastination precedes financial failure. Savvy Money Magnets understand one fundamental principle and that is they cannot afford the high cost of waiting.

Example: The cost of procrastination

$100 per month at 12 per cent
Start saving at:

Age	Total at age 65	Cost of procrastination
25	$979,307	$ nil
26	$873,241	$106,066 (979,307 – 873,241)
30	$551,083	$428,224 (979,307 – 551,083)

The above values are for illustration purposes only and may be subject to applicable taxes.

Here is another way to look at the critical nature of time. Imagine that you are currently 25 years old and have set a retirement goal of $100,000. If you started today by investing only $10.22 per month (that is a mere 33 cents a day) at 12 per cent you would have the $100,000 by the time you are 65 years old. If time passes you by, like it does to so many people, and at age 55 you decide to set the same $100,000 retirement goal, you would have to save $446.36 per month. That is 43 times what you would have needed to save per month if you had started back when you were 25. The point is, regardless of your age resolve today to put time on your side by investing immediately!

All glory comes from daring to begin.

– Anonymous

The Rule of "72"

The second critical element is the rate of interest that the investment will yield. The higher the rate of interest, the better the return. That is common sense. But to fully appreciate the impact that interest rates have on your future wealth let's examine the Rule of "72."

The Rule of "72" states that your money will double at an approximate point determined by dividing 72 by the rate of interest.

The following chart illustrates this phenomenon called compound interest.

The Rule of "72" in Action – Your Money Will Double in...

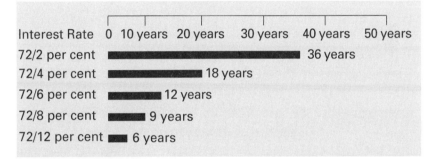

Interest Rate	0	10 years	20 years	30 years	40 years	50 years
72/2 per cent				36 years		
72/4 per cent		18 years				
72/6 per cent	12 years					
72/8 per cent	9 years					
72/12 per cent	6 years					

Beat the Taxman ... Pay Yourself with Retirement Savings Plans

Most countries have financial vehicles set up that allow you to save for your retirement. They are known variously as Individual Retirement Accounts (IRAs) or Retirement Savings Plans. They amount to the same thing. Encouraging you to save for your retirement will take the pressure off future governments, so they allow you to make money within a plan without having to pay any taxes on the gains ... for a while.

When you open an account and make a contribution, depending on local laws, that amount may be deductible against your taxes. Inside the plan, you invest in any of the traditional options: Stocks, mutual funds, CDs etc., but as opposed to investments made outside a plan, any profits, dividends or gains made are not subject to taxation. Over the years of contributing – the longer the better – you gain from compounding without losing any part of it to taxes. When you retire, you should have a substantial nest-egg on which to draw. When you start to take money out of the plan it will be treated as income and you will pay tax.

Many companies have plans to which you can contribute and they will automatically deduct the funds from your pay check. Individuals without access to company plans can set up their own plans. Some companies will even match an employee's contributions. Even if your company has a plan do not become complacent. Keeping all your eggs in one basket can be a disaster if that company goes bankrupt which even the biggest companies occasionally do; Enron, please step forward.

Annuities offered by insurance companies can operate in a similar fashion. They come with much higher fees but without the contribution limits of IRAs. If you opt for this route, hold it outside your plan.

The following chart illustrates the massive long-term benefits of investing money in an IRA.

Comparison of an IRA vs a Non-tax Sheltered Savings Investment

Each person deposits $4,000 per year, at an interest rate of 12%. Both are in the 40% income tax bracket.

	Person A Non-Sheltered	Person B ROTH IRA
Value at year 10	67,824	74,678
Value at year 20	195,744	306,616
Value at year 30	452,123	1,026,981
Value at year 40	965,966	3,264,324

Explanation of Above Chart

The case of Person A illustrates the limited wealth accumulation available in a non-sheltered savings investment. Because he or she is paying tax on all profits, a 12% yield (profit) to someone in the 40% tax bracket would effectively leave the person with only a 7.2% profit.

After 40 years of investing the total will only be $965,966. Not that this is an insignificant amount. It IS significant and, it is certainly far greater than what the average person has to retire on. But look at Person B. **By investing the same amount of money in a retirement savings plan, he or she would have accumulated over three million dollars. A $2,298,358. bonus!**

A retirement savings plan such as an IRA is a very important aspect of wealth building that almost everyone can take advantage of. Local laws vary widely on contribution ceilings and options so we encourage you to research this area as soon as possible. The quickest, easiest advice we can give you is to consult a reliable investment dealer, set up a plan and buy some "no-load" Mutual Funds to get started.

10 Most Common Investing Errors

1. Putting Your Eggs in One Basket.

Picking investments can be a bit of a "crap shoot". Not many people foresaw the high-tech meltdown of 2001, the bankruptcy of Enron, or the economic crisis of 2008-2009 that claimed Wall Street legends such as Bear Stearns and Lehman Brothers. A diversified portfolio stands a much better chance of weathering economic storms such as these.

2. Past Performance is Not a Guarantee of Future Performance

Just because one approach worked once, it is no guarantee that it will work a second time. Watch out for funds that advertise huge past returns over a short period of time. The chances of them repeating their little miracle are slim to none. However, if you notice a fund that has consistently outperformed the market average over a period of ten plus years, then this fund has an established track record and should be seriously considered. If you buy into the fund, monitor it. Often the brain behind the fund's success will be hired away by another firm, leaving your fund in the hands of someone that may not be as qualified or creative.

3. Line of Greater Fools

Often times in a bullish market people get so wrapped up with excessive optimism that they look favorably at an overvalued stock and justify the purchase by saying something like, "It doesn't matter how much I pay for it, I can always dump it off to another buyer." Then the tide turns, bad news creeps into the media, companies cannot sell off bulging inventories and layoffs occur. Despite the writing on the wall, the last investor ignores the warning signals and hopes that his or her declining stock will quickly bounce back. Panic selling hits the markets and share prices drop. This situation can be best described as a "line of fools." The problem is that the last fool in line eats the majority of the losses caused by previous optimism.

4. Hot Tips Will Burn You

Beware of people who have "inside information." The Internet can be a treasure trove of information but beware of the schemes, cons and rip-offs that are propagated. A good question to ask the source of the tip is when and how much he invested. Avoid newsletter tips that focus on predictions. Instead, go for financial writers (newspapers, magazines and investment newsletters) that offer research and information. Avoid telephone and other direct sales solicitations; these are generally not reliable and also come loaded with high fees. *We cannot emphasize this enough: If it sounds too good to be true, it probably is!*

5. Never Let Your Emotions Rule You

Be honest with yourself. If you are the type of person who will become emotional with every rise and fall in your investment's valuation, face facts and get out of the game. It will save your health. Investing in the markets is an exercise in logical thinking. It requires a cool, reasoning head, not someone who will get attached to a specific stock. Rational people do not get all teary-eyed when they switch bank accounts to gain that extra half per cent of interest, so why should emotions by allowed to rule your wealth building decision-making process?

6. You have Got to Know When to Hold and When to Fold

Like in the card game, poker, smart players know when to get rid of losing cards. Likewise, smart investors know when to dump losing stocks and they have a predetermined formula to do so. This will be covered in more detail in the following section.

7. Short-term Fever

This happens when temporary downturns in the market spook investors. The key is to realize that, historically speaking, given enough time the markets always bounce back stronger.

8. Paper Gain or Loss is Not the Same Thing as Reality

Regardless of the current valuation of your stock no profit or loss happens until you cash out. So, it may be disturbing to see your portfolio value drop by ten per cent owing to extraordinary market conditions, but you have not lost anything unless you panic and sell. Similarly, if your stock has risen 200 per cent in value, do not start spending the money. You only realize that profit when you sell. It may be the time to sell that stock and reinvest in other companies before your original pick drops back to a more realistic level. What is the right time to do this? That is the million dollar question. No one has the guaranteed answer no matter what they tell you. Seek the best professional advice you can get to stack the cards in your favor.

9. Cash is Not Always King

Studies have shown that people tend to hoard cash for too long when the market is depressed. Cash reserves are great for comfort and security but lousy for making money. In fact interest rates on cash reserves normally cannot stay at par with inflation.

10. Bigger Risks Equal Bigger Profits

Not always. By having the right advisor plan your portfolio you should be able to increase your returns and reduce your risk.

Denis and Alan's 10 Rules for Investment Success

If you want to try the stock market, understand that maintaining a portfolio can involve a lot of time and research. This is fine if you really like the market but not so good if you do not. It should also go without saying that stocks are risky. Profit potential is historically high over time but any company can suffer huge losses and take you down with them. Be cautious, do the research, diversify and get a good advisor.

If you want the gold, understand Denis and Alan's 10 Rules for investment success:

1. Review the income statement and balance sheet.
2. Assess demand for the company's products or services.
3. Assess the senior management team.
4. Validate the messenger. Before accepting the message (a hot tip or "inside information") consider and validate the source. Will someone directly benefit if you invest? Do they have your interests at heart? Are they knowledgeable and trustworthy? Are they succesful?
5. Assess the potential internal and external risks that could negatively affect the company's performance?
6. Assess how much money you are prepared to flush down the drain without losing sleep. Never invest more than this amount in high-risk investments.
7. Cut your losses. Set a predetermined drop–sell rate; the rate of ten per cent is most common.
8. It is all in the timing. Make your profits when you buy stock at the right price, realize your profits when you sell at the right price. Know when to buy and sell.
9. Invest in your backyard. Invest in companies and industries that you understand and are interested in.
10. Maintain some level of cash reserves.

Simple Guidelines for Choosing the Best Financial Advisor.....and almost Everyone Needs One

Pay your broker well if he or she performs. It is funny to note how Money Minimizers gladly pay 15 per cent for lousy service at a restaurant yet will gripe at paying a broker four per cent.

They overvalue people that serve their liabilities and undervalue those who service their assets. The ideal financial advisor that provides you with a comprehensive, individualized plan for free, and that they get paid their comission as your portfolio grows. You want to develop the discipline of sticking to the financial plan. You don't require a large amount to invest, the point is to start as soon as possible and contribute regularly, increasing contributions as your income grows.

The best way to assess a potential advisor is to judge them on the education they provide. Beware of awards as these may have been earned through the number of clients they have processed. That is not a measure of their success. Get references. Sales people can confuse you with figures and percentages. What does another individual investor say about this advisor? Has he or she made them money? Does this person treat them with respect? Does he or she always take their phone calls or return calls promptly?

The worst places are those with high fees, weak performance and any conflict of interest. Beware the trader who is doing unnecessary trades to build up his or her commission base.

Compare your portfolio results with friends and family. Here is a low-cost source of information, which provides comparisons of how 450 newsletter portfolios perform each month. For 20 years Mark Hulbert of Hulbert Financial Digest (www.hulbertdigest.com) has provided his subscribers with the reality of how well various advisors perform.

An Investor's Bill of Rights

As the investor, you are playing with your money. Therefore,

- Pick an advisor who puts your interests first.
- One who understands your specific needs, wealth building objectives and your tolerance for risk.
- One who will not try and sell you something because it has a higher commission level.
- One who will regularly review your portfolio to ensure it is performing to meet your long-term needs.
- One who has the education, background and track record to offer proper advice.

- One who responds quickly to answer your queries, treating even the most naive in a respectful manner.
- One who will provide you with a regular, clear and understandable record of the progress of your investments.
- One who will be there in person when the policyholder dies, rather than passing you off to an 800 number.
- One who will help you further your own financial education.

If your financial advisor fails this Bill of Rights, then it is time to find a new one.

None of the following investment vehicles give you any real control or influence over their success. You can only control whether to invest in them and the timing of buying and selling. Here is a very basic primer on places to park your money. The list moves from safest to riskiest.

Savings and Checking Accounts

A savings account is a step up from keeping your money in a cookie jar because it is safer. Through the Federal Deposit Insurance Corporation a deposit of up to $100,000 is guaranteed by the U.S. government. Caution: Make sure that your financial institution is covered by the F.D.I.C. and if you live outside the U.S. check your financial institution's deposit protection system. The savings account pays a small amount of interest, the benefit being that your money is very liquid. A checking account allows you to easily distribute your money to other people by writing checks, with the added security of not walking around with cash. Denis and Alan's rule of thumb: Savings account balances should not exceed more than one month of living expenses. Excess money should be invested in higher interest-bearing investments.

Certificates of Deposit (CDs)

A fully guaranteed instrument that pays higher than savings or checking account rates. It is locked in for the full term ranging from 30 days up to five years. Denis and Alan's rule of thumb:

Have two 30-day CDs each at the value of one month's living expenses. The first one should come due on the 14th of the month, the second due on the 28th of each month. That means with the savings account and the CDs, you have three months' emergency fund and at most you are only two weeks away from being able to cash a CD.

T-Bills

Treasury Bills are government IOUs issued for a term of one year or less. You do not receive interest; rather they are purchased at a discount. For example, you buy a $10,000 one-year T-Bill for $9,400. The minimum amount you can purchase is $10,000 with increases of $1,000 thereafter.

Government Bonds

You are loaning money to the government, which they will pay back at a predetermined time and rate of return. Some governments offer a tax incentive tied to the issuance of bonds.

Money Market Mutual Funds

This is a higher yielding investment that is not guaranteed but still very safe because of its conservative nature and stability of capital. Mutual Funds are a means for thousands of people to pool their investment money and are managed by dedicated portfolio specialists.

Stocks

With stocks, you are purchasing shares of ownership in a corporation. You share in both its profits and losses. You can get money by selling at a profit, plus some shares also provide income in the form of dividends.

Mutual Funds

Allows you to pool your money with many others to invest in a broad range of securities. These are managed by experts that carefully monitor the performance of the investments in their

specific portfolio, allowing you to sleep at night while they track the vagaries of the Nikkei exchange at 3 a.m. In theory these "experts" will do a better job than most in picking the better performing securities. They do, however, make mistakes. After a very prosperous year, managers are often enticed to run other funds. In the meantime, the original fund is advertising how well they did in the preceding year, which entices others to invest. The reality may be that the original manager has left and the fund is in the hands of someone about to pursue a less successful strategy, leading to single digit, or worse, returns. Some smart investors pay less attention to the make-up of the portfolio and more to following successful managers from fund to fund.

Most Mutual Fund companies advertise themselves as being *no load* which means that you pay no upfront fee to purchase them. *Back loaded* means that you pay a fee when you sell the fund unless you keep your money in for a specific amount of time, typically three to seven years. That does not mean these are the only fees you pay. Remember, there is no such thing as a free lunch. All funds have a Management Expense Ratio or MER. This is the amount the company charges for administering and selling these funds. These fees come off the top and typically range in the two to three per cent area. So, if your fund says it returned six per cent this year, it actually made closer to nine per cent before the management took its fees. Even if your fund only returned one per cent, the company still took its fee. The person that sold you the fund also got paid out of this expense charge. There are some funds that charge very low fees, from one to one-and-a-half per cent, and can afford to do so because they avoid the expensive advertising campaigns. These are, by definition, harder to find and may only deal with portfolios of $25,000 and above. The other way to avoid making fund companies and their sales staffs rich is to invest in Index Funds.

Sector Specific Mutual Funds

These are mutual funds that deal in specific industries (such as Electronics, Technology, Bio-technology, Computers, Telecommunications, Utilities, Multimedia, Precious Metals and Minerals, Healthcare, Insurance, Food and Agriculture, Air Transport, Automotive, Defence and Aerospace, Energy, Financial Service, Bio-Medical, etc.). The danger is the volatility of placing all your eggs in one sector basket.

Corporate Bonds

You are loaning money to a specific company which they will pay back at a predetermined time and rate of return. If the company goes broke before the payout time, you lose.

Index Funds

How to outperform the money managers? At the beginning of every year our local financial paper gets a group of stock picking experts to list their recommendations for the next 12 months. At the same time they have someone throw darts at a list of stocks, or get a three-year-old to select a portfolio. The three-year-old and the dart thrower invariably do as well or better than the group of experts. What this indicates is the unpredictability of the markets and the element of guessing used by experts. Which begs the question: If a three-year-old can, on average, equal or better the experts, why should you pay an expert for their advice? Chances are, child-exploitation laws aside, the three-year-old will come cheaper and the dart thrower will probably only cost you a beer or two. Cheaper still and as reliable as anything else, are Index Funds.

Until the technology meltdown of 2000–2001, anyone who invested in an Index fund such as the S&P 500, beat 80 per cent of the returns of all fund managers. And, they paid only 0.25 to 0.50 per cent in management fees. So, what is an Index Fund? Well, it is basically a yardstick. The S&P 500, for example, is a group of 500 large companies' stocks, which account for something like 80 per cent of all stocks traded in the America. The index measures their collective performance. The Dow Jones' index measures the stocks of a narrower group of 30 active, large companies. It is possible that an individual stock was up 20 per cent on the same day that the Dow was down ten per cent because it is reporting an average.

With an Index Fund you can take an amount of money

and purchase a proportional piece of each basket of companies. The management team of an Index Fund is a computer, which costs much less to maintain than a group of Harvard business graduates. The upside of an Index Fund is the low fee and the returns which, on average, outperform the highly paid experts. The downside is that there is nobody watching on your behalf for a meltdown or market correction. Index funds are not great performers in bear markets such as the one we've been in for the past few years. An actively managed Mutual Fund will cost more but MAY see a meltdown or correction coming and rebalance the fund to protect your money, or MAY react quicker once the market troubles begin. Lots of fund managers do neither. If you are in for the long haul, putting part – not all – of your portfolio in an Index Fund is a great, low-cost bet.

Collectibles, Precious Metals, Commodities and Penny Stocks

As long as there are groups of people with shared interests there will be a market for collectibles. This allows you to invest in an area that you are passionate about. The caution is that to make

WEALTH POTENTIAL INVESTMENTS OVERVIEW

Highest wealth-potential investments:
Collectibles, precious metals, commodities, penny stocks

Pros	Cons
Huge profit potential	Massive potential to lose. Very complex knowledge required. High levels of taxation.

High wealth-potential investments:
Stocks, sector-specific mutual funds, corporate bonds

Pros	Cons
High profit potential	High degree of risk.
Income-tax reduction opportunities	High levels of personal taxation.
Professional advisors available	High degree of knowledge required.

Moderate wealth-potential investments:
Government bonds, money market mutual funds

Pros	Cons
Quite safe and secure	Moderate rates of return.
Professional advisors available	Capital tied-up for long period.
Registered mutual funds reduce taxes	Non-registered ones are taxed at personal rates.

Low wealth-potential investments:
CDs, T-bills, savings or chequing accounts

Pros	Cons
Very safe and secure	Lowest rates of return.
Very simple to understand	Often principal is "locked in".
Can purchase direct from bank	Non-registered ones are taxed at personal rates.
Registered CDs attract low income tax	

any money, you need to be extremely knowledgeable about the subject area and the collectibles should have long term value. Like collectibles, precious metals, commodities and penny stocks are a very volatile world in which unforeseen events can affect the investment dramatically.

Denis and Alan's rule of thumb: Do not play in this potential minefield unless you really know what you are doing and can afford to lose a great deal of money in a very short period of time.

In this chapter we have given you some strategies to make yourself richer by using your existing assets more effectively. The most immediate means is to leverage the time and energy spent at your job and make it more lucrative by increasing your skill-set, granting you more security and qualifying you for raises. For the more aggressive pursuer of wealth this involves getting a better position either at the current employer or at a new company. Any of these moves should bring you more money, and combined with what you have learned from the preceding chapters, allow you how to manage the extra income much

better. Then you are on your way to a healthier financial future. The second form of leveraging is investing and in this chapter we have given you some options on how to take the money from your raise or savings and have it work more effectively for you. Following the model of this book the strategies go from conservative to higher risk. Choose the risk level that best suits your personality and remember that the more aggressively you pursue these strategies, the richer you will become over a shorter period of time. The third form of leveraging involves using your assets to build new sources of income – an MSI – which will be covered in detail in Chapter 7.

To summarize what we have talked about, here are a few helpful questions to review.

1. What does leveraging have to do with creating wealth?
2. What is the difference between spending and investing? Why is the distinction so important for my financial future?
3. What are the three forms of financial leveraging?
4. Which of the three methods provides the greatest potential to create true wealth?
5. Am I receiving the best possible return on investment from my four personal assets?
6. What changes can I make to fully leverage my job?
7. What conclusions did I make as a result of completing the Decision Tree Exercise?
8. How can I use the information from the Employment Leverage Indicator to maximize my job return?
9. What investment strategies will I pursue to make my money earn an even greater return?
10. How will I ensure that I do not fall prey to one or more of the ten most common investment mistakes?
11. Do I need a financial advisor? If so, how do I find the right one?

The next chapter outlines some of the fundamental behaviors that everyone needs to adopt to be at their most effective level for generating money. After years of study and leading thousands of seminars we have distilled the essence of what you absolutely need to know. Taking the full seminar or reading more books on

The Behavior for Developing Wealth Wisdom, Working Less and Making More

This chapter focuses on the behaviors for developing wealth wisdom. Whether you are planning to maintain your current job, become an investor or start your own business, there are certain behaviors that will make your goals easier to obtain. If you invest some time on the behaviors we talk about in this chapter your life will become easier. If you choose to build your wealth aggressively you will need to adapt these behaviors into your life-style. If you can truly master these skills you will be on the fast track to creating extraordinary wealth.

The Development of Selling Skills for Money Magnets

Time Mastery

"Time Management" is a commonly used expression. If we examine the words it implies that we can actually manage time. The reality is that each human on the planet only gets 24 hours each day, and once you remove sleep, work, family time, meals, commuting, housework, sports, hobbies and other necessary daily routines, most people find there are few available hours left over. We feel that the only management one can do is "self-management as it relates to time". It's impossible to squeeze more hours out of each day. It is, however, possible to get more results out of the hours you have. By managing ourselves more effectively with respect to time, we can greatly increase our accomplishments within a given time frame. There are three categories of activities that fill our 24-hour days. We call them The ABCs of Time Mastery:

- Achievers
- Builders
- Crushers

Achievers are those key activities, which are responsible for most of your money making success. Money magnets understand the fact that only about 20% of one's daily activities contribute towards 80% of their financial success. The key is to note which 20% are the real achiever activities and focus on accomplishing those first.

Builders are necessary obligations that contribute only 20% towards ones financial success, yet if allowed to can occupy most of the average person's day.

Crushers are time wasters such as disorganization, forgetting things and searching for lost items. They contribute nothing towards one's success. The most common and dangerous crusher of success is procrastination.

Take a few moments and photocopy the "Making Time Work for You" chart on the next page. Fill it out and see if you can see how to manage your time more effectively. Even small changes can provide large benefits you will enjoy.

Date: _____   **Making Time Work for You Chart – Sample**

Activity	Time Invested	Specific Wealth Goal	Category (ABC)
Breakfast	30 minutes	Identify or read about new MSIs	A
Commute to job	45 minutes	Organize day's activities*	B
Watching television#	3 hours		C

*Organizing your day will allow you to hit the ground running when you get to your place of work.

#We recommend eliminating two to two-and-a-half hours of these and replace this time with reading something constructive.

Date: _____   **Making Time Work for You Chart**

Activity	Time Invested	Specific Wealth Goal	Category (ABC)

The following activities are priorities of Money Magnets; let's make sure we focus the majority of our daily efforts on them: weekly budgeting, financial goal-setting and implementation, wealth planning, training, self-development, self-renewal, becoming more organized, focusing on building client relationships and spending time with family and friends. Use a time-planning system. Whether it is computer based or paper based does not matter, just use it. A $10 daily planner works just as well as a $1,000 personal digital assistant. When people in seminars ask us which is the best, we always say that "the system that is *used* is best."

Networking

So, you have a great idea that you are passionate about and think will make money. How to put it into action? You could cold-call relevant businesses in the hope of an appointment and ultimately a sale, but you may have to wait at the end of a long line of similarly interested people. Think about it from your own perspective. Generally, people like doing business with people they know. Though your idea may be brilliant, chances are making it a reality will involve someone taking a chance to give you a loan or a purchase order. What if you end up being unable to deliver on your promises? That may leave the buyer or lender vulnerable to other losses. People will be more likely to take a chance and actually help you through some of the rough spots that you may not have anticipated if they know and like you.

Networking can help you in this and many other situations, including getting a job. Many people are relatively shy by nature and not comfortable approaching perfect strangers. Stopping people on the street may not be the safest or the wisest thing to do, but that does not preclude speaking to someone you see every day at the bus stop or in the laundromat. A simple, non-threatening comment about the weather or the local sports team may be rebuffed, or it may lead to a promising conversation. The place to practice this skill is any forum dedicated to the path you wish to follow.

Let's say you want to start a line of clothing accessories.

If you hear about a fashion convention or annual meeting of a department store, this could be where you could make a golden acquaintance. The point is, you just never know what that stranger does for a living. He or she may turn out to be an astrophysicist and is not the least bit interested in clothes, but he or she may just as easily be a huge fan of your favorite band or sports team. You never know and it costs you nothing to find out. Now let's imagine that the woman you keep seeing bringing her son to the same baseball practice as you happens to be the head buyer for a clothing chain. Even if she is not interested in accessories, chances are that she can give you the name of someone who is, or at least will allow you to pick her brain about unknown areas such as distribution, marketing or reasonable sales margins for products such as yours.

In this situation, the first thing you need to have is both a business card and what is known as the '30-second business card.' If you do not know someone, after the small talk ends and it comes down to "What do you do?" you'd better have a good answer. A long description of your fantasies for success and a huge business empire may take longer to explain then that person's attention span. Try to come up with a good description of what you are, or want to be in a few brief sentences. For example: "My name is Melissa. I am the manager of the XYZ clothing outlet at the Uptown Mall and I have just finished the design of a line of fashion accessories for pregnant women." If the person you are speaking with has any interest or experience in that field, they will respond and you take it from there.

Here are a couple of things to remember in networking:

1. Do not be afraid of people. The worst they can say is "No."
2. Always be polite, you may be asking them for a favor.
3. Never knock the competition. Taking the higher ground will win you more respect and you never know if the head buyer for the competition is standing next to you and interested in your idea. The competition could actually be a personal or professional friend of the person you are speaking with. You never know, so play it safe.

4. Do not oversell in a social situation. Just because the person has a professional interest in the type of thing you do does not mean that he or she wants to speak about business in their spare time. You also want to avoid seeming too eager or too desperate. Try and make a positive impression and exchange cards in order to set up a further conversation.

5. Do not back people into a corner, it may backfire on you. If the person is, potentially, a good contact, try and get a brief meeting or offer to buy them a coffee. If they are really busy and do not want to make time for you, let it go. You may meet them again in the future and you want the memory to be a good one, rather than have them run and hide if they ever see you coming.

Developing Profitable Sales Relationships

According to our research, 73 per cent of all self-made millionaires are directly involved in selling. They are either successful, high-commission earning, full-time sales professionals who invested their money well over a long period of time or they are business owners involved in the sale of their goods and services among many other daily responsibilities. Before we proceed any further it would be a good idea to share our definition of selling: **Selling is the process of influencing or persuading someone to your way of thinking.** When you examine this very generalized view of sales, you quickly come to the realization that everyone is involved with some form of selling on a daily basis. Take, for example, a husband and wife who are trying to decide which movie to go see. He may be interested in the latest action flick, while she is dying to see the new comedy that everyone in the office has been raving about. The best "salesperson" will influence the other and thus determine which movie is viewed. If you want to see effective salespeople in action hang out with some small children as they are natural sales people. They are positive, creative, enthusiastic and persistent sellers. When a child wants something and needs an adult to "buy into" the idea, he or she can be very resourceful in trying to influence others into their way of thinking. One of the biggest shames is that all too often society negatively conditions these little salespeople to the point that they lose their natural sales ability. Once this occurs many people find it very difficult to re-connect as an effective salesperson. This explains why our sales training programs are always sold-out.

There are several other reasons why many adults are not as effective in selling as they could be. One of the most significant is the bad reputation selling as a whole has in most cultures. When you mention sales to the average person, he or she usually equates this with a negative process, something that you do to someone. Images of manipulative, slick, pushy and sometimes even dishonest "used-car salesmen" stereotypes come to mind. The reality is that sales, like any profession, has both honest and dishonest players. The act of selling is neutral, it is neither positive or negative. What makes the difference is the intentions of the salesperson. Is he or she trying to gain something at the expense of the customer or are they focusing on a true win-win situation. The professional, high integrity salesperson believes that **selling is something you do *with* someone not *to* someone**. The negative, hard-sell approach salesperson has the personal slogan that they could "sell ice to the Eskimos." The problem with this hard-sell slogan is that the salesperson will in effect do everything in their power to force a product or service on a customer even when there is absolutely no requirement for it.

Another problem type is the order taker. This person's orientation to sales is "no selling." They offer no real advice or options to the customer. They passively wait by the telephone or cash register to process the next transaction. The problem with this approach is that the customer never feels that the individual or the company is interested in him or his business. Companies and their sales staff are missing out on golden opportunities to service all the needs of the customer, making them more satisfied with their buying experience, while increasing revenues.

The final problem type is the "will-not-sell" style. These people believe that selling is beneath them. With indignation in their voice you can often hear them say, "I did not go to university just to become a salesperson, after all I am a professional." Even professionals need to sell if they want to succeed in their practices. Successful doctors, lawyers and accountants all sell. They do not use the hard-sell method; rather they develop relationships with their clients.

The best way to look at sales is the relationship selling method. It is a positive, proactive, long-term, high integrity, win-win method of professional selling. The overall premise is that if you focus your energies on building a trust-based relationship with your potential customers, you will be able to identify whether your products and services meet the needs of the buyer. For the potential buyer to become a customer he or she must possess the following three elements (A, N and D):

Ability – The ability to purchase the goods or services with cash or credit.

Need – The bona-fide need for the good or service.

Desire – The desire to do business with the seller and the company he or she represents.

The first two elements, Ability and Need, cannot be created by the seller. They must already exist within the buyer. The buyer could have a real need for something and not be aware of it. So the salesperson's task would be to create awareness, but not create the actual need.

The key to relationship selling is for the seller to focus on building the buyer's desire to purchase from them. Relationship selling is not manipulative, mysterious or magical. It is the most effective and natural way to sell.

Since the focus is on the real needs of the buyer, the dialogue is based on open, honest, two-way communication between the buyer and seller, with the seller doing most of the listening. One way to remember the importance of listening during this process is the rule of 30/70. This means that to be truly effective in building a positive relationship, the seller should limit his or her talking to 30 per cent of the conversation, while listening at least 70 per cent of the time. This affords the opportunity to truly learn the needs and motivations of the buyer while actively building the relationship.

> God has given man one tongue and two ears so that he can listen twice as much as he speaks.
>
> If you are talking, you are not listening. If you are not listening, you are not learning.
>
> – Lyndon B. Johnson

Another great rule in relationship selling is "Ask VS Tell." This one reminds us that if we are doing all the telling, then we are hard-selling. If we are asking positive, respectful questions then we are actively learning from the buyer.

The following diagram, by Bill Gibson (www.kbitraining. com) illustrates the six natural phases involved in relationship selling. It is referred to as "natural phases" because as soon as you successfully complete the first phase, it is natural and easy to proceed to the next and so on. However, if you try to gloss over a phase or skip it altogether, the process will come to an abrupt halt.

Six Natural Phases of Relationship Selling

1. Targeting Prospects
2. Rapport Building Uncover Buying Motives
3. Presenting/Demonstrating Benefits, Advantages and Solutions
4. Overcoming Objections
5. Closing the Sale and Collecting the Money
6. Turning One-time Buyers into Life-time Customers

Phase One – Targeting the prospects

This is the proactive phase where the seller chooses which specific potential buyers to invest their time, energy and money into developing a relationship. The best approach is to set up a criterion by which to rank various prospects into A, B or C categories. A stands for the absolutely critical potential client for the growth and success of the company. B is for the beneficial one and C represents the convenient one. Possible criteria could be potential sales volume, profits, credibility of the client's name, client's ability to refer new business or entrance into a new market.

Phase Two – Rapport Building and Uncovering Buying Motivators

The basis of relationship selling is the ability of the seller to build a rapport with the buyer very early in the sales process. This can be accomplished by focusing on the buyer's needs vs the seller's. The seller should ask many questions which open the buyer up to sharing what their real needs, challenges and opportunities are. One rapport-building technique that helps bond the two parties together is called matching and mirroring. In this technique, the seller takes the communications style lead from the buyer. This is done by the seller observing the buyer's style of verbal and nonverbal communication. If the seller notices that the buyer is sitting with a formal posture and is speaking in a low, slow voice, then the seller should "mirror" the buyer's body language and tone of voice and respond in a similar manner. The point is not to mimic, ridicule or make fun of the buyer; rather it is to respect the style of communication that the buyer has chosen for that situation and attempt to make them feel comfortable by communicating using the same style. This approach, when used correctly, places the buyer at ease and starts to build a sense of trust between both parties. With the emergence of trust and open dialogue, the seller will be able to learn the buyer's primary motivators which will affect the buying decision.

Buying motivators can be expressed in many ways, but the two primary ones that influence every adult buying decision are: the avoidance of pain or the attainment of pleasure. If the seller can learn how his or her product or service can help the buyer avoid some pain and or attain some pleasure, the likelihood of building the relationship and closing the sale will be very high. Some "pain" issues for them are potential losses, missed opportunities, stress and high costs. Some "pleasure" issues for buyers are increased profits or gains, a sense of freedom and personal enjoyment. It is vital that the seller learns which primary buying motives the buyer is operating from.

> Nothing great was ever achieved without enthusiasm.
>
> – Ralph Waldo Emerson

Phase Three – Presenting and Demonstrating Benefits, Advantages and Solutions

Once the seller has developed rapport with the buyer, determined his or her real needs and uncovered the buying motives, he or she should present and demonstrate the benefits, advantages and unique solutions that his or her goods and services can provide the buyer. At this stage, because of the development of the relationship, the buyer is prepared to listen to what the seller recommends. The seller, by this point, is much better prepared to express his or her solution in terms that are more meaningful to the buyer.

Phase Four – Overcoming Objections

During the presentation and demonstration phase, the buyer may have several objections which will need to be dealt with before moving forward. The main thing to remember about objections is that they are a normal part of sales communication. They are not a negative issue, they simply indicate that the buyer is either unclear about what the seller said or that he or she does not see the value in the seller's offer. An objection is not a "No"; it is merely an opportunity for the seller to re-communicate his or her position.

Phase Five – Closing the Sale and Collecting the Money

Once all of the buyer's objections have all been successfully and positively dealt with, the next natural phase is to close the deal. Sometimes, buyers need a gentle nudge to close the deal. It can

take the form of the seller saying something like, "It seems to me that we have agreed on all the key points so I guess the next step would be to sign the contract." If the seller's interpretation of the situation is correct, the buyer will happily agree to sign the contract. If the buyer still resists signing it is because the seller misread the buyer's willingness to buy and needs to take a step backwards and deal with any unresolved objections.

Phase Six – Turning a One-time Buyer Into a Lifetime Customer

Most people think that once the sale is closed, the process is over. In reality, the relationship selling process has just begun. A common error made by companies all over the world is that they invest virtually all of their resources in trying to gain new business and nothing on retaining their key accounts through effective, proactive customer service. It takes approximately five to seven times as much time, money and energy to create a new customer as it takes to keep an existing customer happy. To our way of thinking, the smart money is placed on servicing your existing customers. In turn, they will become repeat buyers and refer additional business your way. Here is an interesting statistic: each unhappy customer will, on average, tell ten other people; every satisfied customer will tell three other people. The old adage is true: The best (and worst) form of advertising is word-of-mouth.

For more information on our customized sales and business development seminars and consulting services, please refer to our website: www.abcguys.com.

NEGOTIATING IS AN ESSENTIAL WEALTH BUILDING SKILL

Negotiation skills are vital to your success as a Money Magnet and they are critical in accomplishing the win-win objective. Conserving or maximizing money for you and satisfying the other person is the mark of a successful negotiation. Without negotiating skills, you might own a company that has large sales volumes, but your profits could be very small. All the work that goes into a sale, such as: the preparation, developing the relationship, uncovering the buying motivators, the presentation and demonstration, handling of any objections and even a good close, none of these is going to be effective without negotiating skills because you may unnecessarily leave half the profit lying on the table! After all that work, you might as well take the highest profit possible.

Proper negotiations result in the biggest profits. It is the ability to satisfy the other party while maximizing your profits.

Effective negotiators need to have the following skills:

- Product and customer knowledge
- Communications skills
- A positive attitude
- Strong personal organizational skills
- Self-discipline
- Creative problem solving
- An understanding of human behavior
- Knowledgeable at negotiating tactics and strategies
- Developing long-term business relationships

Negotiating is a learned skill. As an ability, it is like playing golf, it flourishes with practice. Granted, some people have more natural negotiating ability than others, just as some people have more natural athletic ability. Like any game, once you know the rules and practice, you become better. We are including the following rules, designed primarily for salespeople, because we are trying to prepare readers for working in their own businesses. These principles, taken in a wider context, are the same ones that you will use when buying a car or a used lawn mower at a garage sale.

Denis and Alan's Nine Rules of Negotiating

Rule #1: Negotiation is a Process, Not a Stand-Alone Event

Most negotiation programs are based on manipulation, gimmicks and underhanded tactics. Most work once! Which is okay if you never have to deal with that customer again. In truth, you will in all likelihood have to deal with this customer again in the future, not to mention all of their friends and contacts. Professional negotiating is based on building value and developing profitable long-term relationships, instead of relying on tricks and gimmicks. The process of negotiating begins at the first phase of the natural sales cycle described earlier in the chapter.

After each encounter, the buyer should see you as bringing more value and integrity to the relationship. He or she sees you either as a business ally, dedicated to helping them solve their problems, or as the enemy, looking to put something over on him. That is why negotiating is a process and not an event. It is a constant evolution of the critical relationships that determine your customer base. If you do not handle the situation fairly, you damage the relationship between the customer and the company at the cost of future business. On the other hand, if you give in when you do not have to, you are training the customer to erode your profits.

Rule #2: Information is Everything

When going into a negotiation, you cannot have too much information. Information equals power and if you enter a negotiation without information, you are in a deficit position. One lesson good business people understand, is that no deal stands alone. Each party brings their history, their personality and style, their prejudices and opinions to the table.

You want to know:

- What does the buyer value?
- What are their needs?
- What do they want and why do they want it?
- What have been their past dealings with your company?
- Who is your competition in this deal?
- What did they like about past dealings with your company?
- What did they not like about them?

Rule #3: Eliminate the Surprises

What additional preparation could you do to avoid any negotiating surprises that the other party could spring on you? What situation could be created that might give the other person more negotiating leverage? What "hot buttons" does this person have that could trigger a negative emotion within them? What competitive advantage could a competitor have over your business that could be used against you?

Rule #4: Know Your Strengths

What competitive advantages do you have over your competition? Why should the other person want to do business with you?

Rule #5: Commit to a Win–Win Philosophy

Why is this deal in the best interest of both parties? How important is it to use this deal as an opportunity to further develop the relationship? What can you do to ensure that you reach a win-win deal?

Rule #6: Do Not Judge a Book by it is Cover

Never underestimate the abilities or negotiating power of the other person. The moment you begin to underestimate them is the moment that you start to erode profits.

Rule #7: Draw a Line in the Sand

Know your boundaries before starting the negotiation process. Have an absolute minimum or maximum dollar figure that you will accept. Work out the possible consequences of hardball action in advance so that if you are forced into making a decision, you do not damage the relationship and regret it later. Identify your line in the sand beyond which you are not prepared to compromise. This is the point where you are prepared to walk away from the negotiation.

Rule #8: Learn from the Past

Review how well you have performed in previous negotiations. What could you do differently next time? How can you improve both the bottom line and the relationship?

As we said before, "If you're alive, you're in sales." This chapter is meant to help prepare you for the arm-to-arm combat of the game. You should now be prepared to negotiate better deals, use your time more efficiently and effectively, and successfully conclude sales more often. Here are some review questions for some of the fundamentals.

Rule #9: Learn From Others

There is huge value in tapping into the experiences of a coach or mentor who has "ben there and done that".

CHAPTER SUMMARY AND QUESTIONS

1. What time wasters can I eliminate from my life?
2. What time obligations can I make more productive use of?
3. How will I accomplish this?
4. Which time priorities do I need to invest more energy in?
5. Am I committed to updating my "Making Time Work" chart daily?
6. When do I commit to start using this chart?
7. Who would I like to meet and what would I like to learn as a result of networking?
8. Am I comfortable seeing myself as a "salesperson"?
9. If no, do I see the value in developing my selling skills?
10. If yes, what specific steps will I take to enhance my ability to sell?
11. From a selling prospective, what does A.N.D. mean and how could mastering this principle assist me in achieving my wealth-creation goals?
12. Which steps within the six natural phases of selling do I need to improve upon? How will I accomplish this?
13. How can I improve my negotiating abilities?

All of the behaviors we have described in this section build on the fundamental changes in attitude from the first section. The various behaviors we have discussed are like rungs on a ladder.

Knowing how to set new goals, living more frugally, organizing your budgets and your time; learning how to improve your skill sets as they relate to your job or interacting with the wealthy and using leveraging, networking, negotiating and selling skills are the most effective methods to move yourself up the ladder of success and wealth.

For those with a more aggressive nature and much higher financial goals, moving up the ladder is too slow a method. Their wealth goals demand different tools for advancement. Wealthy people want to accumulate their wealth quickly with minimum physical effort. They use the ladder method for as long as it takes to get their bearings and experience, then switch to the elevator. The element that turbo charges the entrepreneurial elevator is creativity which is the third section of this book. The more gradual steps of the ladder are most appropriate for the majority of people who are just learning the principles of the entrepreneurial mindset. For more aggressive money-makers – ones who wish to create extraordinary wealth quickly and are not averse to taking some calculated risks – using the ladder method to wealth exclusively is simply the "rung" approach.

> You always pass failure on the way to success.
>
> – Mickey Rooney

The final chapter outlines the path to a much richer future. It calls for an even more aggressive personal campaign, but pays off with much greater financial rewards. Again, we will take you from conservative to riskier behaviors, the rewards being commensurate with the amount of energy and action taken. Though the risks are greater, Chapter 7 will show you how to reap the rewards of the truly rich.

SECTION III

CREATION OF MONEY

7

CREATING EXTRAORDINARY WEALTH WITH MULTIPLE SOURCES OF INCOME

Once you have corrected any wealth-limiting attitudes, cleaned up any bad budgeting or credit behaviors and set aside a regular deposit for investment purposes, you are ready for the following specific, easy-to-achieve strategies that will move you into the land of the wealthy.

The most compelling reason to invest time in this section is the fact that 74 per cent of self-made millionaires own their own businesses. Sure, everyone has heard a story about some seemingly penniless person living in a near derelict building that turns out to have left a fortune of several million dollars at their death. They are examples of people who have simply taken the frugal behaviors described in Chapter Four to obsessive lengths. These exceptions aside, all wealthy people either inherited their money (or a family business) or, more likely, engaged their own creativity and started their own companies. Bill Gates (Microsoft), Michael Dell (Dell Computers), Steve Case (AOL), Colonel Harland Sanders (KFC), Ray Croc (McDonalds) and Warren Buffett (Berkshire Hathaway Investments) are just a few obvious examples.

Creativity is the sudden cessation of stupidity.

– Dr. E. Land, Inventor of Polaroid

This is the section that some people will have the most fun with, while others will consider it the most challenging. Multiple Sources of Income (MSI) is about diversification. This might be, simply, an extra stream of income in addition to your day job. You may turn that one additional income into your full-time pursuit, or you may end up like the true entrepreneur and have several streams of income. It depends on your level of interest, time and energy. The greater creativity you invest, the wealthier you will become.

Denis writes: "Until Alan and I met roughly 14 years ago, Alan made most of his income as a producer/writer for national radio and television programs, events and documentaries and as a broadcast consultant. I was primarily a professional speaker, trainer and financial adviser. We met while consulting the same client, a broadcaster in the process of setting up a network. I was involved in the staffing and financing areas while Alan's focus was programming and management.

"When we met we quickly recognized each other's entrepreneurial streak. It was not long before we agreed to use Alan's skills as a writer and producer to help me develop and produce a series of special television programs aimed at building self-esteem and entrepreneurialism in teenagers. After discussing our complementary skill sets and common philosophies of business, we agreed to work on some financial consulting projects together.

"Alan had taught himself to be financially prudent but had only applied this knowledge to his own situation or that of friends and family. Working with me as a financial consultant was initially, therefore, a bit of a stretch for him and the challenge was intriguing. Similarly, despite my years in front of the camera, I had not worked on the production side of television and was anxious to learn the techniques. Most importantly, neither questioned whether each had the abilities necessary to work in these new areas, we simply agreed to do whatever it took in terms of self education to be able to properly execute whatever project we chose. Although neither of us had previously identified either of these as growth areas, we were each able to recognize a golden opportunity when it arose. Each of us had the ability to work beside experts in their field and learn from them.

"Unfortunately, many people either fail to recognize opportunities or they assume that they are not capable of working in unfamiliar areas. That can be a fatal assumption and, as they say, when you assume, you make an ASS out of U and ME. The only assumption typical of the Millionaire Mindset is that they can achieve virtually anything if they put their mind and energies into it.

"The risks people like us take in producing television programs or devoting time to writing books, provides employment to cameramen, photographers, editors, studio owners, production assistants, printers and many more. Part of the reward for taking these entrepreneurial risks is that we benefit from certain tax advantages unavailable to fully salaried people. We each run our businesses out of our homes and deduct a portion of our household expenses from our taxes. The telephone bills we generate in the furtherance of the businesses are fully deductible, as is the purchase of computers and other supplies. Since we live in different cities, the costs incurred in getting together for meetings are deductible.

"The other important element is that we have agreed to work (whether independently or as partners) only on projects we feel passionate about and deem to be fun. We believe that the two most important things money brings are independence and freedom. As a result, we have turned down many potentially profitable projects. Our personal goal is not to have more money than everyone else, but rather to enjoy the time we have. And not everything we do is principally to make more money. The self-esteem for teenagers project, for example, is built on an excellent economic model. Sponsors not only reap tremendous community awareness values but actually stimulate greater sales in the process. We make money on these projects but in this example, the primary beneficiaries are the kids. We made the decision to set the project up this way only because we both felt that ventures like this are desperately needed today.

"When we decided to put our research and experience into this book project, we decided that this would require a few weeks away from the distractions of home life with telephone calls, faxes and e-mails constantly vying for our attention. So we arranged to spend time at various luxury Caribbean resorts and got to work. As we sat around the pool in our 'off-time' researching the attitudes of fellow resorters we were reminded that we both enjoyed the process of our work very much. It did not hurt that as 90 per cent of what we were doing was work, if we had actually paid for the trips instead of taking them in trade, the costs of the trips would have been fully deductible.

"We each independently took the plunge to making ourselves rich many years ago. Do we each have exceptional skills? Yes. Are they ones that no one else could develop and use for their own success? No."

> There are enough business opportunities available to facilitate everyone in the world becoming a millionaire.
>
> – J. Paul Getty

Try this simple self-assessment tool:

The ABCs of Making Money – Entrepreneurial Quiz

Instructions: Read the following 10 statements, answer "true" or "false" to each as they apply to you.

Part One: Entrepreneurial Indicators

	True	False
I have a burning desire to be successful.	___	___
I believe that failure is not an option.	___	___
I get so focused on my goals that I often forget everything else.	___	___
I believe in the saying, "If it's to be, it's up to me".	___	___
I am passionate and energetic about winning in life.	___	___

I respond well under situations of pressure and stress.   __ __

I believe that taking reasonable risks is what life is
   all about.   __ __

I don't focus on problems; I see challenges
   and opportunities to conquer.   __ __

I am seen as an entrepreneur by others.   __ __

I am a positive, action-oriented person who is
not afraid to dream.   __ __

Interpretation: Each "true" rating is worth one point. A combined score of 8 or higher demonstrates an entrepreneurial attitude that can serve you very well as you consider embarking on your entrepreneurial journey. If your score is below 8, continue re-reading the chapter then try the quiz again. Some of the stories may inspire you. If you still score lower than 8 then concentrate on the strategies in the B section of this book as that is how you will be most comfortable and successful.

Part Two: A Partial List of Entrepreneurial Skills
As a potential business owner, you should have a solid understanding of the various facets of running a successful business. Do this self-assessment exercise to gauge your entrepreneurial skills. Upon completion use the "No" and "uncertain" items and embark on a process to enhance your skills.

Entrepreneurial Skill	Yes	No	Uncertain	Area to Improve
Buying things at a low price	__	__	__	__
Making stuff	__	__	__	__
Organizing	__	__	__	__
Quality Control	__	__	__	__
Problem Solving	__	__	__	__
Using computers	__	__	__	__
Decision Making	__	__	__	__
Leading People	__	__	__	__
Keeping costs low	__	__	__	__
Bookkeeping/ Budgeting	__	__	__	__
Understanding Customers	__	__	__	__
Selling at a profit	__	__	__	__

Providing quality Customer Service	____	____	____	____
Advertising/ Creative Promotions	____	____	____	____
Staff Selection and Training	____	____	____	____

YOUR INTERESTS: A SIMPLE SELF-ASSESSMENT TEST

Do you need a university education or years of specialized training to start your own business? Absolutely not. You may already have most of the knowledge that you will need. The first step then is to spend some time on self-assessment. We are going to walk you through the simplest of tests.

For each of the following questions write down your top three answers.
1. What jobs are you trained for?
2. What jobs could you do if you had just a little more training?
3. What job could you do if you absolutely had to (if someone became ill and you were the only person available)?
4. What are your dream jobs (forget the training needed and the qualifications, what would you really enjoy doing)?
5. What are your interests, hobbies or leisure activities? For example, travelling, collecting antiques, cooking, shopping, organizing events or surfing websites.
6. What subjects are you most comfortable discussing (construction, sports, music, wine, etc.)?

By reviewing these answers you should have a fairly good picture of what you are (or could easily be) qualified to do. Now ask yourself:
1. Could you imagine yourself setting up your own company to do one of the jobs you have just identified?
2. Is there a demand for that job?
3. What would you need to set up such a company in terms of

financing and other resources? (We will get more specific on what you need to set up a company later in this chapter.)

4. Does this involve a day-to-day life-style that you are comfortable with? For example, someone who is not by nature a people person may find it very difficult to go out everyday and talk up their business with strangers. The opposite is also true. Someone who loves being and working with people may hate working alone out of their home office.

5. Is it realistic?

USING YOUR EXISTING TALENTS AND RESOURCES TO CHANGE YOUR LIFE

Rosa, a single mother of two young children, was depressed and at her wits end. She had barely been surviving on her government Mother's Allowance benefit, when her financial roof caved in. Her youngest child had fallen seriously ill and required numerous costly treatments. (Happily, the child eventually recovered from the illness.) Unfortunately, Rosa's debt-load and day-to-day expenses were becoming far too much for her to bear. This had not always been the case for up until six months before, Rosa had been employed as an assembly line seamstress until she was laid-off after the plant's closure.

Since the layoff Rosa had actively searched for employment but owing to her limited job experience and low formal education, the only job options seemed to be minimum wage. Rosa would have gladly worked at any job just to get back on her feet. However, a minimum-wage job would not cover childcare expenses and pay the bills, let alone the medical debt. Rosa's situation was further compounded by the fact that she had no immediate family to help her.

After seeing our self-esteem television show, she decided that her past was not going to equal her future. She immediately took out a piece of paper and started to write down her various assets. After analysing her current situation from a different perspective, she decided to contact the local university to see if any student would be willing to baby-sit the children part-time in trade for free accommodation. One of Rosa's assets was the three-bedroom apartment that she rented. The children could share one room, which would free up the third room for someone else. After meeting several interested students she finally settled on a second year, Early Childhood Education student, who jumped at the opportunity of reducing her costs.

Rosa was now in a position to once again seek employment. She found a part-time job as a seamstress at a department store. The pay was a bit higher than minimum wage and she did not have childcare costs. Rosa quickly learned how to measure people's new garments to make final alterations after the purchase. After working several months, Rosa got the idea to approach various small clothing shops that lacked an alteration service. She would demonstrate the correct method of measuring garments to the retail staff; then, at the end of each day she would collect the garments from various retail clients, do the alterations on her own home machine and return them two business days later. Within several months the business was growing and people were asking Rosa to do sewing repairs as well.

It got to the point that Rosa simply could not keep up with the workload so she contacted some of her former co-workers, most of whom jumped at the opportunity to work part-time on a piecemeal basis for Rosa. She then went to the receiver that handled the closing of the plant who happily sold her five industrial sewing machines at an unbelievably low price. Rosa supplied each of the women with a sewing machine, for which she charged a monthly usage fee, enabling her to pay off her loans. Within a short period of time Rosa had more than tripled her former monthly wage plus she had the added bonus of reducing her taxable income with the various costs of doing business. She had also improved the lives of five of her friends. One night, her student boarder lamented that she wished someone would design a stronger, more affordable student backpack, one that would outlast the cheap nylon version that kept ripping under the strain of her third-year textbooks. Rosa, once again, saw and seized the opportunity. She and the student designed several backpacks made of spare denim material that was lying around. The resulting backpack was durable, fashionable and very inexpensive to produce. The backpacks sold very well at the university bookstore and at several city outlets that catered to the student market. The net monies earned from the backpack venture did not make Rosa rich, or place her into early retirement. It did, however, give her a way out of a seemingly desperate existence, restore her sense of self-respect and help pay off her medical debt in less than four months!

> Give me a stock clerk with a goal and I will give you a man who will make history. Give me a man without a goal and I will give you a stock clerk.
>
> – J.C. Penny

As we mentioned earlier in this book, it is an absolute shame that two-thirds of senior citizens are not able to retire to an independent life-style. Here is an example of how a retired couple decided to change their financial life. Alex and Mira's situation was that Alex had changed many jobs during the span of his working years which prevented him from building an employee pension fund. Nor had the couple built a large retirement nest egg. Alex had retired at age 65 and within two months had started to receive his old age pension from the government. Two years later, his wife turned 65 and she too qualified for the pension. Almost five years later they realized that at the rate they were going, they would easily outlive their diminishing savings. Advertisements depicting a sun-splashed, comfortable retirement amounted to cruel taunts to this couple. Their small monthly pension just did not cover the basic costs of living and as a result he had to work part-time on the "graveyard shift" as a security guard at a warehouse. He described the job as "mind-numbing monotony, where you froze in the winter and baked in the summer." His monthly after-tax pay was $1,000. He and his wife turned to us and asked: "When does the gold become part of our Golden Years?"

The only real asset the couple owned was their house, situated in a modest blue-collar neighborhood on a double-sized lot valued at around $200,000. Although they had the equity of the house they did not want to sell it and move into a rental.

They reasoned that they had worked hard for 30 years to pay off that mortgage and they valued the principle of real-estate ownership. We suggested various alternatives to consider. One suggestion we made seemed to resonate with them. That was to sell their house and instead of living from the principal, to invest the proceeds into purchasing a larger house with a much smaller yard. The rationale for this idea was that the smaller yard would require less effort to maintain and the municipal tax base was, to a large extent, based on the number of square feet in the property. This move would result in saving several hundred dollars a year in taxes. We also suggested that they buy a house large enough so that it could easily be subdivided into four separate units and the dwelling zoned appropriately.

After researching the market they eventually found the right house and made an offer of $165,000 (conditional on the sale of their house). Their house sold six weeks later and they netted $192,500 after legal and real-estate fees. They hired a contractor friend of theirs to do the necessary work to convert the new single house into four units. Because they had purchased a house that was easy to convert and got an excellent deal from their friend, the total cost for the renovations was only $35,000. That meant that for a net cost of $7,500 (on their line of credit at 6.5 per cent), they now owned a four-unit building. They lived in one unit on the ground floor and rented out two units for $600 each per month. The fourth unit was a bachelor apartment in the third-storey loft. Although they could easily get $400 per month they decided to let a responsible, handy, young single man have it for $200 if he would act as the building repairman should anything require attention. The result was that within the first six months they had paid off the $7,500 line of credit, Alex had quit his job, they had less yard work and housecleaning responsibilities, a substantial asset, plus an additional source of income of $1,400 per month!

Rosa and Alex and Mira's stories illustrate how people in seemingly hopeless (their term) situations managed to turn them around using only a little creativity. They did not go back to school for years of retraining or win the lottery. They simply used their existing assets more effectively. They did not become fabulously wealthy but they are now much happier and are beginning to think entrepreneurially. Who knows where they will grow next?

> Everyone who's ever taken a shower has had a business idea. It is the person who gets out of the shower, dries off and does something about it who makes a difference.
>
> – Nolan Bushell, Founder of Atari

MAKE YOUR LIFE EASIER AND EARN MILLIONS

Is there something you would love to see invented that would help you in your day-to-day life or at work?

Consider the story of Bette Nesmith Graham. At the age of 17, Bette took up a job as a typist in a company. In the 1950s, before the advent of computers, letters were typed page by page and if you made a mistake, you had to retype the whole document. When electric typewriters became popular, correcting mistakes with a pencil eraser resulted in ugly smudges and ultimately required retyping.

One day Bette observed a painter who corrected his smudges and flaws by painting over them. Inspired, she grabbed a can of water-based paint and tried covering over her typing mistakes back at the office. It worked. By 1956, Bette's solution was so popular that she was making batches of what she was calling "Mistake Out" in her kitchen. Recognizing the need she applied for a patent and changed the name to "Liquid Paper."

Evidently there were a lot of other mistake prone typists as by 1979 the company she created was selling 25 million bottles around the world annually and providing employment for 200 people. Satisfied with her accomplishments she sold the company that year to the Gillette Corporation for $47.5 million. Not bad for a poor typist.

You are never too young for success

Kelly Reinhart was an average six year old when her mother asked her and her siblings, just for fun, to draw a picture of

something that would be useful as a new product. Kelly had seen shows of cowboys who wore holsters to carry their guns. So, she drew a picture of a thigh pack perfectly suited to holding her portable video games and cartridges. Kelly's parents thought it was a good idea and helped her make one. When she wore it to school the next day she was the envy of her friends who each asked her to make them one. Thinking ahead, Kelly incorporated her friend's comments and feedback into the design for a prototype, which her parents produced with the help of an associate. After supplying her school friends, the Reinharts tried their luck at a local flea market and quickly went through the initial 100 they had brought. The next step was the trade shows in Atlantic City and Las Vegas. After a little research they found that their state government offered a free referral program to match entrepreneurs with appropriate financiers and marketing experts.

While her parents worked out marketing and distribution logistics Kelly approached the US military through her Congressman. Following a meeting with the US Secretary of Defence and various military experts at the Pentagon, Kelly's idea is being adapted to military use and they are considering offering her a research and development contract.

Not content with that, Kelly has started a foundation for kids who wish to pursue their dreams, and authored a book called *This Little Pack Goes to the Market*, which she hopes will help kids realize that "every idea is a good idea."

"The advice I can give to other kids is to let their parents or an adult know that they have an idea" Kelly said. "If the adult does not pursue it, then put the idea in a folder for a later day until [the child is] old enough to bring it up again or when they know who to approach."

The next step on Kelly's agenda is becoming a Senator "so I can help people and educate them on the process of business and help make it easier to find money for making dreams come true." Kelly is clearly an exceptional child. But, are not all children exceptional? Put your child on the payroll as an idea incubator and get ready for retirement!

Turning Your Hobbies into Wealth

Let's go back a few pages to the Self-Assessment Tool and look at your interests and passions (questions four to six). Ask yourself the following questions.

1. Is there a market for what you are most interested in? Let's say you love wine and are reasonably knowledgeable about it. Could you start a newsletter or write for a newspaper or magazine (tip: Start small, perhaps on a community paper level; do not worry about getting paid initially, this is good practice, good exposure and will prepare for your entry into a paid position) or start to import from other countries and sell to restaurants and liquor outlets? Or, if you like to ski, travel and organize events, you might want to create and sell ski charters; or if you are interested in photography and enjoy meeting and working with people, perhaps a videotaping service would be right for you.

2. Could you set up a part-time business in your home and run it, at least initially, after work and on weekends?

The point of this exercise is simply to determine your strengths and interests and determine if any of them has the potential to be turned into a second or third stream of income.

Meeting a need, whether it is informing people about a good buy in wines, or manufacturing a product that people want or find useful, even on a part-time basis, can immediately change your financial position in a significant way. Working out of your home while continuing to hold down a job offers the security of a pay check while you see whether your idea can sustain itself in the marketplace. If it does, then when the time is right, you can leave your job and devote yourself full time to your idea. If it does not meet your expectations you still have your job and pay check, you will have learned some invaluable lessons about how businesses are set up and run and, most importantly, for the period of time that your business is in operation you can write off part of your living expenses.

We will walk you through the reality tests for your ideas shortly but first here are a few examples.

Robert is a skilled mechanic working with imported cars. He is a good worker, good with his hands, creative and also loves working with wood. With two young kids in a small house, clothes were everywhere, particularly in the winter. He went to his garage workshop and built an attractive shelf under which was a series of pegs which would hold coats. Installed at the front door, it solved the problem of the coats and sweaters on the floor and provided a place for gloves and hats. Everybody who came to their house admired the utilitarian design and workmanship and asked him to make them one.

Naturally this got him to thinking about other things he could build for the home that people would want to buy. His wife encouraged him and while he started sawing wood, she set to work researching new markets. Soon they were regulars at community events and fairs where they would rent tables to display their goods. While they both enjoyed the experience, it was not tremendously lucrative. There was a ceiling on how much they could charge for individual items if they did not want to end up carting everything home at the end of the day and, when they took into consideration the cost of materials, his time to manufacture and her time in marketing, there was not enough left over to make it worthwhile. He could have sold his products to a distributor but, again, the time needed to build compared to the wholesale price he could charge was not worthwhile. However, through the sales he made at the community fairs, he received plenty of requests for custom work designing and building. Now, through word-of-mouth referrals, Robert builds everything from cabinets to backyard decks, which earns him a comfortable living doing something he loves. He is also able to write off part of the expenses for his house, truck, telephone and his new computer, to name a few. (See Storyboard Action System, page 189.)

On a recent trip to Sweden we met a woman from England whose story certainly demonstrated some inspirational elements. Dianne was working in an office until she suffered a horrific car accident while on vacation in Australia. After three months in a coma, doctors finally revived her. She lost all use of her right arm and her memory had been badly damaged. Faced with

The ABC's of Making Money
Storyboard Action System

Multiple Source of Income Idea:
Converting My Woodworking Hobby Into a Profitable MSI.

Date: _____
Project Leader: _____

Wood Products	Services	Customers	Inventory	Tools and Equipment	Bus. Set-up	Mrk/Sales	Financial Issues		Channel of Distribtuion		
Wood Toys	Repairs	Family / Friends	Supplies Needed Possible Suppliers	Workbench	Determine Business Structure	Professional Referrals e.g. Real Estate Agent	Set-up Sales Procedures Terms		Workshop/ Font Lawn		
Furniture: shelves, tables bookcases	Custom Orders	Neighbours/ Community	Compare Suppliers	Shelves	Registration Bus./Bus. Name	Signage Displays	Breakeven Analysis		Retail Stores		
Decks	Contractor	Retail Shoppers	Negotiate Account/Terms	Wood Racks	Meet Banker Current Account	Client Testimonials	Profit Analysis		Table Fairs/ Markets		
Furnishings: Coat rack Cutting board	Teach Woodworking	On-line Buyers	Order Initial Supply	Commercial Van	Book Keeping System	Word of Mouth	Cash Flow Analysis		Catalogue		
Spice rack		Mail order Customers	Create Inventory Control System	Power Tools Sander, Drill Circular Saw	Obtain Tax Numbers	Brochure Catalogue Packaging	Financing Options For Growth		Internet		
Garden Shed		Wholesalers Distributors	Location of Warehouse Storage Space	Hand Tools Hammer, Axe Chisel	Select Workshop Space	Bus. Card letterhead	Pricing		Contractor/ Broker		
Fences			Receiving Supplies		Write Bus. Plan	Vehicle Signage			Wholesaler		
					Obtain Stationary/ Supplies	Portfolio of Previous Work			Shipping Prices/Terms		
					Select Bus. Advisors Mentor/Friend Consultant	Work Order Contract					
					Start-up Capital	Sales Representative (Spouse ??)					

this trauma many people would not have had the courage to continue. Dianne saw it differently. She enrolled in an Australian college and learned to speak English again, albeit it with a strong Aussie accent. When she finally made it back to England she decided to study computers, becoming so proficient that she was hired as an instructor. One of the problems she had to overcome was the inability to hold down keys with her left hand while operating the computer mouse with her right. She solved this by fashioning something like an oversize pencil, which she holds and operates between her teeth. After quite a bit of practice she now operates a computer much quicker than either of us.

The rehabilitation hospital in which she convalesced got her used to the idea of using adaptive devices, enabling her to cut bread and slice vegetables with one hand. Extrapolating from this example she has fashioned several devices of her own, which, for example, allow her to handily beat visiting consultants at billiards. Some of these devices she builds herself, or has them built for her and she sells them through local rehabilitation hospitals.

Dianne makes a good living teaching computer skills. She could start to market her adaptive devices around the world, however, she is not out to make millions of dollars. Having had a very close brush with death she now values every minute she is alive. She is happy to share her devices with those in need. The extra income she derives pays for holidays in the sun and the purchase of a new, specially designed motorcycle to help her travel the world.

Here are three examples of people who have created an MSI while doing their regular job: An accountant, a janitor and a waitress. None of them has made millions of dollars as a result yet. They have, however, significantly changed their comfort levels. Their extra income allows them to write off part of their living expenses, which makes a big difference at tax time. Also, the money has allowed them to set up long-term savings plans and enjoy a higher standard of living.

Our accountant works for the government. That is his Primary Source of Income. In addition:

- He performs private tax returns on off-hours.
- He offers bookkeeping services to three sole proprietors.
- He teaches a ten-hour course on financial management for non-financial types at a community college.
- He is creating a CD-ROM financial template for small businesses to be sold via the Internet.

Our janitor works in a grade school. In addition:

- He performs general maintenance services on a part-time basis to clients.
- He functions as a broker to other people who perform cleaning services for homes and offices.
- He is writing a 'helpful hints for cleaning around the house' book for sale at craft fairs, and subsequently through a traditional publisher.
- He is patenting a new cleaning device that he accidentally discovered in his regular work.

Our waitress works in a restaurant. In addition:

- She works with a friend operating a catering business.
- She has developed a relationship with the suppliers to her restaurant and works part-time as a representative selling their products.
- She is a part-time social event planner (weddings, Christmas parties and various social events).
- She works with alcohol suppliers as a demonstration person to promote new beverages.
- She has used her skills in analysing strong and weak points of restaurants and bars, and sells her skills as a hospitality consultant.

MONEY-MAKING BUSINESS OPPORTUNITIES

Here is a list of various money making business opportunities to consider when embarking upon the search for your ideal business. (*From: Uncover and Create Business Opportunities by Bill Gibson*)

Opportunities with existing businesses:

- Buying an existing business.

- Buying a franchise.
- Franchising your business.
- Find opportunities arising from your current business.
- Imitating successful products or business ideas.

Opportunities in manufacturing:

- Manufacturing under license.
- Rebuilding manufactured parts.
- Assembling products.

Opportunities in invention and innovation:

- Inventing a new product.
- Locating a patent opportunity.
- Combining two or more assets into one new one.
- Transferring ideas from one industry to another.
- Substituting materials in existing products.
- Adding value to existing products.
- Finding uses for waste materials.
- Drawing upon the resources of under-used people.
- Launch an Internet e-business.

Opportunities in specialized supply:

- Identifying market gaps or shortages and filling them.
- Becoming a supplier to another producer.
- Catering to left-behind markets.
- Tailor products for unique client groups.
- Providing a consulting or information service.

Opportunities in marketing and distribution:

- Marketing someone else's product.
- Become a distributor for a product or service.
- Exporting local products to new markets.

Opportunities in trends and events:

- Taking advantage of a market switch.
- Capitalizing on a growth trend.
- Taking advantage of a fashion or fad.

The ABCs 15 Power Points of an Ideal Business

We are constantly asked by would-be entrepreneurs for guidance in selecting the best business opportunities. With such a wide array available we developed 15 points to consider when assessing the potential of a business idea. This list of points should be viewed as a guideline, not an absolute. Generally speaking, the more of the following points that your business idea possesses, the greater its potential for success.

Ideally, Your Business Opportunity Should...

1. Sell to the masses.
2. Fulfill a fundamental need for many people.
3. Be low risk.
4. Provide the opportunity for ongoing passive income.
5. Require a low staff component.
6. Have a stable, growing, long-term demand.
7. Have low overhead costs.
8. Have low start-up costs.
9. Have a unique quality, making it difficult for competitors to copy.
10. Have positive cash-flow and low inventory costs.
11. Have high profit margins and rates of return.
12. Have minimal government regulation.
13. Be portable.
14. Be fun, challenging and satisfying for the business owner.
15. Provide an opportunity to uncover other money making MSIs.

Direct Marketing companies have been around for decades. They offer individuals the opportunity to quickly get into an existing business. The reality is that Direct Marketing companies run the range from illegal pyramid schemes to sound businesses. Prior to signing up with any of these companies it is critical that you invest the time and effort to analyze the business using **The ABCs 15 Power Points of an Ideal Business** above. Be wary of privately owned companies, publicly owned businesses are usually much more transparent. Seek businesses that have

" I.P.O. "

invested in numerous 'Brick & mortar' professional office or retail locations. The companies to avoid are the ones that rely on 'internal consumption'. That is, any company that insists on you buying - they'll call it 'investing in' - thousands of dollars worth of their products, and then getting you to convince other people to do the same thing. The challenge is for anyone to actually sell these 'pills, potions and lotions' to people outside the company. No matter how much better a company claims their products to be, if you can buy a similar product for a much lower price at a place like Wal-Mart, most people will. You're then stuck with expensive inventory that you'll end up throwing in the garbage. Not surprisingly, over 90% of Direct Marketing companies go out of business within 2 years. Our advice: stay away from those opportunities, regardless of their wealth promises.

Do the following analysis for each business you consider:

Business Opportunity #1:
Overview of business:
Pros: Cons:
Score out of 15:

Business Opportunity #2:
Overview of business:
Pros: Cons:
Score out of 15:

After carefully analyzing each opportunity, and scoring it against the ABC's 15 point system, you should be able to see which business is right for you. Now, review the highest scoring

business and ask yourself these last three critical questions:
1. Do people like me succeed in this type of business?
2. Are there the people and the support systems in place to help me succeed in this business?
3. Are there any guarantees or assurances of success that accompany this business?
The more "yes" responses you get to these questions the more confident you can be of achieving success.

After reviewing and analyzing thousands of business opportunities around the world one company that meets all 15 of our criteria is **Primerica**. Primerica has a 33 year proven track record in the financial services industry. Currently this debt free company is ranked #1 in Term life premiums, with over 4.3 million lives insured, and they have over 2 million investment clients, with $31 billion in assets under management. In 2010 they listed on the NYSE and was named one of the most successful IPOs of the year, with its share price increasing 65% in 12 months. Top private equity firm Warburg Pincus invested $10 million researching their business model and said "We believe Primerica is uniquely positioned to be the top financial services distributor in North America." They then invested $230 million in their stock. Primerica has over 100,000 representatives across America and Canada and is currently expanding. From the beginning, the company's philosophy has been to educate their clients to buy more affordable Term life insurance - as recommended earlier in this book - and then to invest the money saved. Their mission, much like ours, is to help families become debt free and financially independent.

We first noticed Primerica because their mission and core business values closely mirrored ours in terms of "Economising, and then investing the savings." They also score points when it comes to setting up an ideal business. For 33 years they've been a leader in providing business opportunities to motivated people, with low start-up costs ($99) low overhead expenses and stable, long-term high growth potential. Apparently it's not uncommon for part timers to earn an extra $1,000 or more per month and over 14% of all full timers make over $100k per year.

Denis and Alan's Quick and Easy Business Idea Questions

(Adapted from Bill Gibson's *Uncover and Create Business Opportunities*.)

Now that you have the idea that will make you millions, take time to go through the following:

1. Write a simple description of your business idea. Be specific.
2. How much money should it be creating for you?
3. What is the product and/or service you will offer?
4. What problems or opportunities will it address?
5. Who will buy it?

Next, answer the following questions by checking either Yes, No, or I Don't Know.

	Yes	No	Don't Know
Personal Considerations	—	—	—
1. Is this idea something I am passionate about?	___	___	___
2. Am I prepared to sacrifice aspects of my personal life to ensure the success of this business?	___	___	___
3. Is the work something I will be excited about years from now?	___	___	___
4. Is this idea legal, ethical and consistent with my values?	___	___	___
5. Will this idea enhance my reputation?	___	___	___
6. Do I want to work with the people who may be associated with this idea?	___	___	___
7. Is this idea better for my needs than others I am considering?	___	___	___
8. Do I have enough time to work on this idea?	___	___	___

Marketing Considerations

1. Would anyone buy this product
   or service at this price?   _____ _____ _____
2. Can I find enough customers
   to support a business?   _____ _____ _____
3. Does this idea have at least
   three competitive advantages?   _____ _____ _____

Production Considerations

1. Can I produce enough of the
   product or service?   _____ _____ _____
2. Can I find the necessary
   production facilities?   _____ _____ _____
3. Can I find a stable supply of
   materials at the right price?   _____ _____ _____
4. Can I find the necessary
   production staff or equipment?   _____ _____ _____

Financial Considerations

1. Can I obtain the necessary
   start-up capital for this business?   _____ _____ _____
2. Can I project a positive ongoing
   cash flow?   _____ _____ _____
3. Will the business' financial
   results meet my expectations?   _____ _____ _____

Reviewing the Results:

For every question you answered "I Don't Know" do your research and then decide between "Yes" and "No".

If there are more than three "No" answers, consider the following:

- Make some basic changes to improve your idea and then test it again.
- File the idea and move on to test a different one.

Three Ways to Begin a Business

(From: How To Start A Business, The Fundamentals by Diane King)
There are three main ways to start a business: Start from scratch, buy an existing business or obtain a franchise.

Start From Scratch

For many entrepreneurs, starting from scratch is the only option. Household resources – space, energy, time and materials – can be used to help get the business established. This is very important when start-up capital is limited. Starting from scratch requires more effort and time than buying an existing business. It can take time for a new business to become known to customers. The start-up and early years can be periods of losses or low income.

Advantages

- You decide what product or service to sell.
- You decide your method of selling.
- You set your prices.
- You choose your location.
- You choose the logo, packaging, merchandising, advertising and promotions.
- You decide how much and when to re-invest in the business.

Disadvantages

- Long start-up period.
- Lack of existing structure and systems.
- Challenge of attracting first customers.
- Sales and income can be irregular.
- You may have to do everything yourself because of limited financial resources.

Buy an Existing Business

Buying an existing business often reduces the time it takes for the business to show a profit because it already has a customer base. Financing may be easier to get than if you start from scratch because of the business' history. The two most common pitfalls are buying an unhealthy business that neither new owners nor new money can revive, or paying too much for a business. (For more on buying an existing business, please see Appendix 2.)

Advantages

- An existing business, with a solid history, increases the likelihood of a successful operation for the new owner.
- The time, cost and energy required doing a thorough planning job for a new business is reduced.
- Financing is often restricted to the purchase and is easier to obtain.
- A successful business will have a proven location.
- An existing business will have an established clientele.
- Sales can be realized immediately.
- Inventory is already present and suppliers are established with accompanying credit lines.
- Equipment is in place and its capabilities are known in advance.
- The owner and employees can pass on their experience to you.

Disadvantages

- The existing location may not be adequate.
- The premises may not conform to modern standards and require substantial improvements.
- The previous business practices may have worsened business relationships.
- Precedents set by the former owner may be difficult to change.
- Certain employees may not be useful to the business, while good employees may leave.
- Lines of merchandise are already established and may not conform to the buyer's long-term vision for the business.
- The buyer inherits any poor public image of the existing business.
- The clientele may not be the right fit and changing the firm's image and market positioning can be very difficult.

- The purchase price can be over inflated, creating a burden on future profits.
- Union agreements may prohibit necessary changes.

Purchase a Franchise

With a franchise you are buying into a proven structure and system with built-in support. This is both the greatest advantage and disadvantage of franchising.

Advantages

- The reputation, branding and credibility of the franchise network.
- The availability of support professionals, management and business training.
- The acquisition of a planned business based on a proven concept.
- Financing at preferential rates.
- Economies of scale in purchasing equipment, supplies and advertising.
- Protected territory.
- Research and development undertaken by the franchiser.

Disadvantages

- Restrictions on the franchisee's autonomy.
- High initial costs.
- Profits shared with the franchiser in the form of royalties.
- Compulsory co-operative advertising based on percentage of sales.
- Limitations on creativity and initiative.
- The consequences of the incompetence of other franchise operations in the network.
- Restrictions governing the sale of the business.
- Some are forced to purchase goods from the franchisee at inflated prices.
- Some franchises do not protect territory.

The single most important thing to consider in all three of

the above scenarios is the importance of research. Inadequate research can cost you your business and your life savings. We cannot emphasize this enough. Talk to everyone you can about the business. You may think your spouse's cooking is the best on the planet but before you invest in the restaurant, invite the neighbors over for dinner then ask them to fill in an anonymous questionnaire. If it is an existing business, speak to clients and creditors to learn whether the business is doing well and what it is doing wrong. You may find, for example, that the company's creditors and suppliers will not extend terms to a new owner. This will alter your financing and projections. Read all the fine print in franchise operations. Franchisers are in the business to make themselves rich, not you. That is not to say there are not good opportunities available, just that you have to be very careful.

Look at the idea from every angle and play "Devil's advocate." Consider the worst-case scenario and how you would react to it. Try and find the flaws before it costs you money. Before you sign on the dotted line have the contract checked by a lawyer and a business consultant or accountant for any potential problems. It is the best money you can spend. You wouldn't buy a house without first having a building inspector check it for problems. Buying or building a business or a franchise amounts to the same thing. Rely on people with more experience to "kick the tires" with you.

Understanding Business Structures

One basic question facing all new business owners is: What business structure is best for me? There are three main types of businesses: sole proprietorship, partnership and limited company (corporation).

Sole Proprietorship

Sole proprietorship is the simplest and least costly to setup and, thus, is the most common form for new businesses. The sole proprietorship is a business that is owned and operated by one person. Most self-employed people operate as a sole proprietorship. As sole owner of the business, the proprietor is personally liable for business contracts and is responsible for any

wrongs committed by his or her employees.

Advantages

- Easy and inexpensive to set up.
- Directly controlled by the owner–operator.
- Flexible, with little regulations imposed.
- Business losses can be deducted from other incomes.
- Wages paid to a spouse are deductible from the income of the business.

Disadvantages

- Unlimited personal liability (which means all personal and business assets of an owner can be taken to fulfil business obligations).
- No opportunity for continuity. The sole proprietorship dies when the sole proprietor goes out of business or dies.
- Narrow management base.
- Difficulty in raising capital.
- Difficulty in selling the business.

Partnership

A partnership is also easy to set up. Two or more individuals come together to create a legally binding business relationship in which each partner takes responsibility and becomes liable for the actions of the other partners. This includes actions that may be taken without a partner's knowledge. A partnership must legally register its name and fully disclose information about all of the partners, so that the public has the means of finding out whom it is dealing with.

Advantages

- Easy to set up.
- New partners can be added easily (so, this structure is more flexible and has a greater chance of continuity than a sole proprietorship).
- Few formal legal requirements.
- Risk is generally shared equally among partners.

- Partners can provide support and complimetary skills.
- More sources of capital.
- Broader management base.

Disadvantages

- Tax and estate-planning options are limited.
- Partners and all their assets – personal and business – are at risk for any losses suffered due to other partner's actions.
- Decision-making may be difficult (because each partner has equal rights to be part of the decision-making process).

Corporation or Incorporated Company (Limited Company)

By issuing shares and following government procedures to incorporate, a corporation has a life of it is own; it can outlive members and shareholders. All shareholders are part owners, able to vote with their holder's equity, which is their share of the business. Legal liability is limited to the amount of the shares owned by each shareholder. Each corporation sets its own rules within the law for shares and business operation.

Advantages

- Limits the amount of legal liability of owners.
- Corporation itself is recognized as a legal entity.
- The enterprise has a continuous existence.

Disadvantages

- Requires a lot of paperwork and regular reporting to the government.
- Expensive to set up compared to other business structures, usually requiring a lawyer's costs and government incorporation fees.
- Less privacy regarding financial and other affairs.

How to Create a Powerful Money Making Advisory Team

One of the most important things to remember in starting a

business is that you instantly become a multi-tasker whether you want to or not. Until you can afford to hire other personnel, and because it is one of the most expensive items in running any business, you will probably need to start off performing a lot of these functions yourself. You will become your own secretary, lawyer, accountant, courier, researcher, public-relations manager and advertiser among other jobs and, at the end of the day, you will also be the one that empties out the trash. Very few people are actually trained to fulfil all of these functions but you will be amazed at how, with a little bit of resourcefulness, you will be able to cope. Once the business starts to grow, you will be able to hire other people to fulfill these functions. The fact that you have at least some experience with these jobs will make you better qualified to hire the best person, more empathetic with the realities of the job and it will be more difficult for anyone to take advantage of you. That does not mean you work in a vacuum. Lots of people, if approached properly, will be happy to give you free advice. Of course, the old maxim "You get what you pay for" is true, so the trick is to choose the right people to help. How do you create a powerful money-making advisory team that will help you accomplish your wealth-creation goals?

Possible team members:
- Your banker
- Your accountant
- Your lawyer
- Your mentor
- Your financial or investment advisor
- Your wealthy best friend

Thirteen Key Questions to consider when assessing the value of a potential money making team member.

1. Does this advisor have more income producing assets than you?
2. Is his or her net worth greater than yours?
3. Is this advisor a good listener, is he or she "tuned into" your needs, objectives and concerns?
4. Does this advisor communicate in simple, easy to understand terms?
5. What is their business, educational and professional

experience; i.e., what are their credentials?

6. Is this advisor constantly investing in his or her own personal and professional development?

7. Is there a record of his or her past performance upon which you can base the soundness of their advice?

8. Will the advisor provide you with a list of references?

9. What is the money-making or wealth-creation process this advisor proposes you follow? Is it clearly laid out for you?

10. Is this advisor tapped into a network of various specialized professional services?

11. What role will this advisor play in the implementation of the proposed money-making or wealth-creation plan?

12. Does this person charge for their advice? If so, how do they charge (commission, fees, percentage of assets or a combination of all these)?

13. Are their charges fair and competitive?

The ABCs Simplified Business Plan

If you are committed to setting up a new business you need some form of a plan. Traditional business plans are very cumbersome and difficult to complete for the average person. So, we have developed the simplest of business plans, if you photocopy and fill in the following charts and invest the necessary time to obtain accurate information, your chance of success will dramatically increase. As you go through this process you will likely uncover potential challenges that need to be addressed before launching your business. The point of the exercise is to eliminate as many surprises as possible and stack the odds in your favor. This plan, albeit simple, is still a very powerful method of communicating the viability of the business idea to a potential partner, investor or lender.

Projected Upfront Costs:	Amount
Business idea research costs	
Cost to develop a prototype	
Business registration/Cost of incorporation	
Permits/Licenses	
Patent/Copyright registration	
Skills/Knowledge upgrading	
Professional memberships	
Insurance	
Marketing Material:	
Business cards	
Letterhead	
Brochures	
Flyers	
Website	
Signage	
Paid advertsising	
Other	

The ABCs Simplified Business Plan (cont'd)

Business Supplies: 　Office supplies	
Raw goods and materials	
Purchase/rent equipment: 　Office equipment	
Manufacturing machines	
Tools	
Other	
Professional fees: 　Bookeeper/Accountant	
Lawyer	
Consultants	
Others	
Facility Rentals: 　Office	
Storage/Warehouse	
Leasehold improvements	
Office furniture	
Other	
Total Projected Up-Front Costs	

The ABCs Simplified Business Plan

Projected Business Costs for Month of:	Amount
Rental/Leasing Office	
Property Management Fees	
Warehouse	
Manufacturing Facility	
Equipment	
Vehicles	
Utilities: electricity/water/natural gas/oil	
Parking	
Janitorial/Cleaning fees	
Financial Charges Banking & Credit card merchant fees	
Interest expenses	
Bad debts	
Refunds or Returned product	
Telephone - Land lines & Cell phones	
Internet	
Advertising	
Cost to purchase or produce goods for (re)sale	
Travel, including accomodations & meals	
Postage/courier	
Sales commissions	
Employee wages & benefits	
Insurance	
Taxes	
Total Projected Costs for month of:	

The ABCs Simplified Business Plan

Projected Sales for Month of:		
Service or Product:		Amount
Service 1		
Service 2		
Service 3		
Product 1		
Product 2		
Product 3		
Total Projected Sales for month of:		

Financial Viability Assessment	
	Amount
Available Start-up capital	
Total projected upfront costs	
Total projected monthly costs x 12	
Total forecast sales for first year	
Net projected surplus or shortfall	

Now that you have completed The ABCs Simplified Business Plan and you have confirmed the viability of the idea, you can now proceed on your own, or you can approach an investor or lender for financing. The only thing you will need to show them is a brief written overview of your business idea. The form on the following page will help you organize your thoughts in this area.

The ABCs Simplified Business Plan
Business Idea Overview

What does this business entail?

What is the business structure (Sole proprietorship, partnership, limited company?

Who are the business owners?

What products or services will be offered?

What experience, skills/knowledge does the business owner team have in this industry?

Who are the prospective clients?

What is the current need for this product or service?

What is the projected future demand?

Who is your competition?

What are your competitive strengths over your competition?

What are the risks? How will you overcome them?

How much of the startup capital are the owners committing to?

What collateral is available to secure the business debt?

What is the investor's expected Return on Investment?

Now that you are thinking entrepreneurially, here are a few stories of companies you may have already noticed.

Learning from Other's Mistakes

When Bernie Marcus and Arthur Blank were laid off after the department store in which they worked unexpectedly closed, they could have applied for government assistance or simply looked for another department store job. Instead, they decided to pool their expertise and open an even better store serving the needs of the handy and not-so-handy man and woman. The way they looked at it, their last employer had given them a paid education. As a result of working in that store they saw what worked well and, more importantly, what did not work. They generated a mission statement, a business plan, borrowed some money and opened a store.

The first store was a modest one attached to another department store and carried 25,000 products. Their vision was of warehouse-sized stores filled with a wide assortment of products at the lowest prices and, most importantly, with trained associates giving absolutely the best customer service in the industry. They maintained a very large, well-trained staff and catered to the weekend handyman. Everyone from amateur to professional was made to feel equally comfortable.

Today, the average Home Depot store is approximately 130,000 square feet and offers between 40,000 and 50,000 products. They are one of the top sellers of lumber in the world. Since starting out in Atlanta in 1979, the Home Depot has grown to encompass 2,258 stores throughout America, Canada and Mexico. Their success is not simply the result of being bigger or cheaper than their competitors. It is because they go beyond their role of supplier to become a knowledge resource for their customers. In doing so they have obviously hit the nail on the head.

When You are Really Good at Something, Tell People You are the Best

Several years ago while working in London, England we met an interesting character whose story shows that almost anyone can achieve their goals if they combine passion and energy. While we were leading seminars, he was in the adjacent hall judging an international competition sponsored by Vidal Sassoon. David Gan was born into a poor rural Malaysian family of eight children. A primary school dropout at age 11, he worked for two years with his single mother as a rubber tree tapper. At 13, he was a shampoo boy with dreams of becoming a hairdresser someday. He moved to Singapore and worked 12-hour days in a hair salon as an apprentice. By 1979, he had saved up enough money to travel to London to obtain his stylist certificate at the famous Vidal Sassoon Salon.

Three years later, he opened Passion Hair Salon with a monthly lease of $2,500. David wanted desperately to be seen as different from the other local stylists. At that time, all the high-end salons had posters of famous Hollywood personalities adorning the walls. David offered to cut and style hair for local celebrities for free if they would agree to have their pictures taken professionally and placed on David's walls. This strategy worked very well, providing instant credibility for David's work and attracting many new clients.

He continues to build his celebrity status and personal branding by appearing often on local television shows and receiving ample print coverage. He is a regular judge at fashion and hair shows throughout Europe and Asia. Remember, this is a guy who never even learned to read. David makes millions of dollars per year doing something that he loves while enjoying the celebrity life-style.

If You Really Love Something, Maybe Others Will be "Keen for the Bean"

It is not that the Starbucks coffee chain brews the best cup of coffee in the world. They make a decent brew but they present and market their product very effectively. In 1971, a couple of coffee aficionados opened a location in Seattle's Pike Place

Market. At a time when most Americans thought coffee came already ground from a can in the grocery store, they took pride in getting the best beans available and made a science of consistently brewing the best coffee possible. The original owners, college roommates at the University of San Francisco, were not trained entrepreneurs. Jerry Baldwin majored in literature and Gordon Bowker was a writer. While living in Seattle they would order coffee beans by mail from Berkeley or take the three-hour drive to Vancouver, Canada where they could buy dark roasted beans. One day, after completing the drive, Gordon got the idea to open his own shop in Seattle. Together with Jerry and one other friend they each invested $1,350 and borrowed an additional $5,000 from a bank. April 1971 was not a promising time for a new venture in Seattle. The region was in a state of economic downturn and coffee consumption was declining. Their passion for coffee, however, was infectious. The three were on a mission to educate consumers about the true joy of world class coffee beans. They were *not* on a mission to build a multinational corporation.

Initially they bought their beans from the supplier in Berkeley but, as the business grew, they bought their own roaster and imported their own beans. The small group of employees at their first outlet could all discuss the taste of the different coffee beans from around the world and how different roasts affected each type of bean. No one talked down to the customers. On the contrary, they believed that their customers were intelligent, sophisticated and prepared to learn more about coffee. Ten years later, their reputation attracted businessman Howard Schultz who became a devotee like any other customer. When he joined the company in 1982 he began marketing the Starbucks brand coffee beans to Seattle's better restaurants and coffee bars. After a trip to Italy he noted the prevalence of the coffee bar culture and decided that they should start the same concept in Seattle. It worked, and the reputation for premium coffee and beans travelled. They opened other retail outlets in cities in America and Canada. Simultaneously, they started offering their products by mail order throughout America, further extending their brand and reputation. Fourteen years later, the Starbucks coffee bar total worldwide is over 4,700. Not bad for flavoured water.

May I Have Another?

Debbie Sivyer loved baking cookies from the age of 12. By her 18th birthday in 1975 she had perfected her recipe for chocolate chip cookies. Two years later, she married financial consultant Randy Fields and would often send him to work with a fresh baked batch of her finest. Poor Randy rarely got the chance to sample the treasures as they were quickly snapped up by clients and co-workers who begged for more. A similarly smitten banker liked the cookies so much that he agreed to loan the couple $50,000 to open the first Mrs. Fields retail store in 1977. After paying down the loan and building up their capital, the second store was opened two years later in San Francisco. Her $450 million dollar business now includes 600 stores worldwide and is listed on the London Stock Exchange. And, she does not spend a dime on advertising. Her success is based on word-of-mouth awareness. Think about that next time you bake or eat a cookie. But don't stop there.

Mrs. Fields has learned her lessons very well and they extend to virtually any business. Her recipe for success is the PPP strategy, standing for Passion, Perfection and Perseverance. She says: "The most important ingredient for any entrepreneur is a genuine *passion* for his or her business." In her case it was a passion for baking the best chocolate chip cookie possible. A great product is not enough. It is the passion for the product that will get you through the disappointing times of getting turned down for loans or any of the other multitude of negative answers that you are bound to hear throughout the process of building a business. Passion is the element that keeps you pushing forward, refusing to accept "No" for an answer until you find someone to recognize the genius of your idea.

Mrs. Fields took the long-term approach with her business right from the beginning. Rather than trying to cut corners and turn a quick profit she believed that *perfection* in her cookies as well as the way she treated her customers was the only acceptable manner of operating. She reasoned that by setting the bar at the highest level, if she occasionally fell short of the goal, the result would still be higher than that of any of her competitors.

The third ingredient is *Perseverance*. Fields remembers the early days of slow retail sales. She didn't just sit in her store waiting for customers. When it was slow, she would walk the street in front of the store offering free samples to passersby. In any new business there will be slow days and disappointments but if it is a genuinely good idea and enough people beyond your immediate family agree with you, the good days will come. Six hundred stores, $450 million, no advertising, you do the math!

Think about it: a decent cup of coffee, a chocolate chip cookie, an electronic game holder. None of these is the cure for cancer. Neither are they a car that runs for 200 miles on a single gallon of gas. These are common, everyday items.

We believe that everyone has a skill, a talent or an idea that he or she could use to make themselves wealthy. We have chosen all of the examples in this book specifically because they involve "average" people as opposed to Harvard graduates with business degrees or scientists equipped to develop the next generation of microchips. An advanced education can open up many opportunities but it is not a prerequisite for financial success. You already have what you need, it is simply a matter of seeing it within yourself. Once you have the idea and you have tested it, if you really have the passion and perseverance, you will attract other like-minded people. Perhaps your genius is simply the ability to recognize the genius in other people. Keep your eyes and ears open and then encourage and invest in that person.

> It is not impossibilities which fill us with the deepest despair, but possibilities which we have failed to realize.
>
> – Robert Mallet

If you would like some help with an idea, we offer free advice to a limited number of people. You can contact us through our website: www.abcguys.com. You'll also find other valuable information, support, templates and links as well as information on our seminars and consulting services. In future books we will tell more stories of people who have traded in their "ordinary" lives for extraordinary wealth. We hope to hear about and tell **YOUR** story in the near future and enjoy your company under the palm trees at a five star resort soon. Good luck!

Appendix 1
Recommended Reading List[1]

As A Man Thinketh by James Allen
Beating the Street by Peter Lynch
Common Sense by Art Williams
Dig Your Well Before You are Thirsty by Harvey Mackay
Getting Rich In America by Brian Tracy
Guerrilla Selling by Jay Conrad Levinson
Incorporate and Growth Rich by C.W. Allen
Marketing Your Services by Rick Crandall
Recruiting & Retaining Great People by Dr. Denis L. Cauvier
Rich By Thirty by Lesley Scorgie
Rich Dad, Poor Dad by Robert T Kiyosaki
Rich on Any Income by James P Christensen
7 Habits of Highly Effective People by Stephen R Covey
Stress For Success by Dr Peter G Hanson
The ABCs of Making Money for Teens by Cauvier/Lysaght
The Lazy Man's Way to Riches by Richard G. Nixon
The Millionaire Next Door by Thomas J. Stanley
The Money Advisor by Bruce Cohen
The 9 Steps to Financial Freedom by Suze Orman
The Wealthy Barber by David Chilton
The World's Greatest Salesman by Og Mandino
Think & Grow Rich by Napoleon Hill
Trump: The Art of the Deal by Donald Trump
Unlimited Power by Anthony Robbins
Unlimited Wealth by Paul Zane Pilzer
Wealth Without Risk by Charles J Givens

[1] These books are suggested readings and the investment advice may be time sensitive. As always, we recommend seeking your own professional, legal, financial and investment advice.

APPENDIX 2
Key Business Investigation Questions for Buying an Existing Business

(From: How To Start A Business, The Fundamentals by Diane King) The following business investigation checklist indicates many of the important questions you should answer if you are considering buying an existing business.

Sales   Yes   No

Will sales of the product be maintained
or improved?

Is the product in danger of becoming
out of style or obsolete?

Are prices competitive?

Are competitors gaining strength?

Are all sales documented by reliable records?

Are the total sales broken down by product line?

Are bad debts deducted from sales, or are they
shown as receivables?

Do you know the sales pattern on a year to year
and month-to-month basis?

Is the sales pattern seasonal or related to some
business cycle?

Are some sales at present just on consignment,
with the right of being returned for full credit?

Are some goods under a warranty?

Are some sales fluctuations due to lucky,
one-time occurrences?

Is a particular salesperson critical to success?

Is the seller's personal role important?

Are you sure all sales are for this business and
that the seller has not added sales from
another business?

What protection do you have against the seller
competing with you?

Will you be able to continue to buy the product?

Can you get licences to sell and or to protect
    any exclusive rights? _____ _____

Can you increase sales with current resources? _____ _____

Costs	Yes	No
Are all expenses shown?	_____	_____
Is there a chance the owner has paid expenses through another business?	_____	_____
Has the owner avoided some expenses that could be delayed, such as equipment maintenance?	_____	_____
Are there annual expenses that are due soon?	_____	_____
Are there new or increased expenses you should anticipate?	_____	_____
Is an adequate salary allowed for work done by the owner?	_____	_____
Is depreciation claimed for the equipment and if so, is it reasonable?	_____	_____
Is the staff adequately paid, or do they expect increases soon?	_____	_____
Does your lease have an escalation clause to include increases in building taxes, heat, etc.?	_____	_____
Do you know what effect decreased or increased sales would have on your costs (and consequently on your profits)?	_____	_____
Do you know what expenses similar businesses in the same industry have?	_____	_____
How would a change in your product mix affect costs?	_____	_____
Are some expenses paid in advance by the seller?	_____	_____
Has inventory been accurately shown for true current value?	_____	_____

Profits	Yes	No
Have you looked at the effect of increased or decreased sales on profit?	_____	_____
Are profits adequate to warrant taking the risk?	_____	_____

Have you considered what effect inflation will
have over the years to come on sales or
on costs?   ____   ____

Assets   Yes   No

Do you know exactly what you are buying
and not buying?   ____   ____
Are there asset lists and have you checked them?   ____   ____
If inventory or work-in-progress is to be
included, has a value been agreed upon at
the time of offer?   ____   ____
Have you agreed on how it will be adjusted
at the time of closing?   ____   ____
Has inventory been sold but not shipped?   ____   ____
Have you decided what intangibles you
want – mailing lists, name rights, etc.?   ____   ____
Can these intangibles be transferred?   ____   ____
Do you know what is involved in
transferring them?   ____   ____
Are you buying the accounts receivable?   ____   ____
Do you know how old they are and the
account history?   ____   ____
Could you sell them off to a third party?   ____   ____
Is equipment in good shape and efficient?   ____   ____
Is equipment in danger of becoming obsolete
or difficult to service?   ____   ____
Can it be sold easily?   ____   ____
Is any equipment leased, do you know the
terms and the cost?   ____   ____

Liabilities   Yes   No

Are the assets you are buying free of debts
and liens?   ____   ____
If you are assuming some debts, do you know
the exact terms of repayment?   ____   ____
Do these assets come with warranties;
are they transferable?   ____   ____

Are you assuming any risk of being liable
    for the previous owner's actions?   _____   _____

Has the previous owner received any payments
    in advance or deposits which should be
    turned over to you?   _____   _____

Have you checked the business' credit rating
    with suppliers and banks?   _____   _____

Will the cash flow be enough to pay your
    operating costs and debts?   _____   _____

INDEX

ABCs Simplified Business Plan
206-210
accountant's MSIs, 190-191
advisory teams, 203–205
Alex and Mira's story, 183–184
Annica and Tim's story, 75–79
annuities, 142
Anthony's BMW Z4, 32–34
assets, 56, 88,119–120, 147,
153, 172–175, 184, 192, 194,
203, 204, 205
attitudes to wealth, 11, 12, 13,
18, 29, 30, 32, 39, 43, 67,
129
  negative ones, 27, 72, 73
  parental influence on, 18
  relation to success, 26

babysitting, 99
bartering, 94
becoming wealthy, 16, 46, 55
beginning a business, 198-199
  buy an existing business,
  198-199
  purchase a franchise,
  200–201
  start from scratch, 198
beliefs about wealth and money,
11,12, 13, 21, 27, 37, 46
beliefs
  self limiting, 20, 45, 67
Black Tar University, 58
blaming and responsibility, 34,
35
blueprint resume, 132
BMW, 32, 33, 34, 98
bonds, 149
borrowing, 101

budgeting, 74, 75–79, 158, 160
business ideas 191-197
  financial considerations, 197
  marketing considerations,
  197
  personal considerations, 196
  production considerations,
  197
  sources, 193
  tests for, 194
business opportunities, 114,
115–116, 119, 191
Business Plan 206-210
business structures, 201–203
  incorporated companies, 203
  partnerships, 202
  sole proprietorships, 201
business cards, 159
businesses, starting your own,
25, 57, 97
buying motivators, 164–165

cable TV, 77, 84, 97
carpooling, 97
cars, 97, 98
cell phones, 75, 84, 93, 94
Certificates of Deposit (CDs),
148
Claire's story, 53–54
Clinton, Bill, 52
collectibles, 152
comfort Zones, 30, 31, 32, 51,
61
commodities, 152
compound interest, 141
computers, 76
consolidation loans, 93
corporate bonds, 150

Get The ABC Guys helping your organization achieve its goals!

The authors of *The ABCs of Making Money* series are committed to helping their clients succeed. Practical, results-oriented training, consulting & professional speaking services are available in the following areas:

- Wealth Development
- Team Development
- Sales & Customer Service Development
- Personal Development

For more information on how **The ABC Guys** can assist your organization please contact: info@abcguys.com

"The senior level consulting, followed by the series of team workshops has helped us through our strategic corporate transformation. We have been exposed to consultants and trainers from different parts of the world, however, the board of directors and the senior management team are unanimous in saying that no one comes close to The ABC Guys in delivering bottom-line results".

Rizal Commercial Banking Corporation

"You guys changed my life."

FS; Fresno, CA

"Excellent seminar! Thanks."

EE; Boston, MA

"Thanks for an incredible day. I came seeking "pebbles of wisdom" and received an amazing value for both my personal and professional life. Thanks guys."

SH; Vancouver, BC

Do we have to watch another generation struggle until they retire below the poverty line?

- Teenagers spent $175 billion last year, an average of $104 per week.
- The majority of students aged 16 to 22 have never taken a class in personal finance.
- Student credit card debt is currently $500 million
- Student loan debt is at $60 billion
- The under 25 age group is the fastest growing group filing for bankruptcy

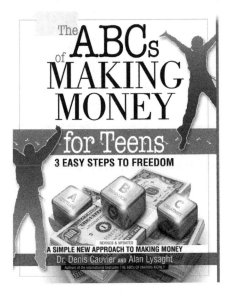

"America's youth will benefit greatly from learning the basics of starting and owning their own business outlined in this great book!"

Fred DeLuca
President and Co-Founder
Subway Restaurants

This street level primer, written specifically for teenagers, will instill an invaluable sense for the power of money and the spirit of entrepreneurialism. It follows the same successful formula as its predecessor, which stresses the importance of Attitude and Goal setting as the building blocks for success in any endeavor. When teenagers are shown that they each have the power to achieve any realistic dream, they'll be empowered to do it!

Full of exercises and games that will instill a notion of planning for the future as well as tips for saving, setting up bank accounts and investment plans and how to avoid getting ripped off by banks and credit card companies.

Most importantly, throughout the book there are lots of inspirational stories of teens who have used their imaginations to start up environmentally friendly enterprises, profit making companies and charities from their basements.

The past does not have to repeat itself
Let's Change A Generation!

Order at www.abcguys.com

ORDERING

AND

VISIT

www.abcguys.com

Also distributed by: